A Handbook for
First Year Teachers

A Handbook for First Year Teachers

Ready! Set! Go!

Memory Long Schorr

Illustrated by
Linda Martin

1995
Teacher Ideas Press
A Division of
Libraries Unlimited, Inc.
Englewood, Colorado

TEACHER IDEAS PRESS
A Division of
Libraries Unlimited, Inc.
P.O. Box 6633
Englewood, CO 80155-6633
1-800-237-6124

Louisa M. Griffin, Editor
Brooke Graves, Copy Editor
Kay Minnis, Layout and Design

Library of Congress Cataloging-in-Publication

Schorr, Memory Long.
    A handbook for first year teachers : ready, set, go! / Memory Long
Schorr ; illustrated by Linda Martin.
    xvii, 169 p. 22x28 cm.
    Includes bibliographical references and index.
    ISBN 1-56308-170-9
    1. First year teachers Handbooks, manuals, etc. 2. Teaching
Handbooks, manuals, etc. 3. Classroom management Handbooks,
manuals, etc.   I. Title.
LB2844.1.N4S36   1995
371.1--dc20
                                                    94-47480
                                                       CIP

Dedicated to my father, Woody, and my beautiful mother, Bernice Long, who were my first and best teachers; to my daughter, Kim, and to my adorable and inspiring grandchildren, Taylor, Memory-Lynn, and Amanda.

Contents

Preface

This manual is for you, the first-year primary teacher. The suggestions and activities it contains may be modified for use with children in preschool through the fourth grade. Specific grade levels are sometimes given where greatest interest and success can be expected. After thirty-five years in the classroom, I have decided to write down many of the things I discovered the hard way after signing my first teaching contract in 1960. Every year I have watched new teachers grapple with the problems and solutions we old-timers take so much for granted. I remember vividly how I tried to look as though I knew all the ropes so I would not seem naive and ill-prepared for my first teaching assignment. I hope I can help you avoid some of the pitfalls and uncertainties that can plague the new teacher.

I suggest you read this manual from cover to cover prior to beginning your first teaching year. Keep it handy thereafter so you can refresh your memory as new situations arise throughout the school year.

My first year of teaching was the fulfillment of a fantasy that began when I was a five-year-old watching my big brother leave each morning for a magical, faraway place called *school*. Throughout my childhood I played teacher, lining up all my dolls and stuffed animals, teaching them everything I learned at school each day. Later, the children I babysat for became my unsuspecting first students. I never lost sight of my goal to become a teacher, and to this day I can think of no other way I would rather live my life.

For most of us, the first year of teaching is the exciting culmination of several years of college preparation. Armed with the best intentions and training of the institutions we attended, we find ourselves alone at last with the awesome task of launching a new school year for ourselves and a passel of exuberant and eager children. During this first year, you may be overwhelmed by the hundreds of small and large details of teaching that no one ever told you about in college or during student teaching. For instance: What do I do about lunch money? Should children take it with them to the lunchroom, or should you send it to the office? How do I handle bloody noses? Where's the tempera paint? Does light duty really mean I turn out all the lights when everyone goes home, or does it mean no heavy lifting? What do I do with the mother who won't leave my classroom? What should I do for my first open house?

Good teachers possess creativity, optimism, playfulness, love of life, and tremendous stamina. These are the characteristics that draw them to the profession. When others speak of job boredom, you will be unable to identify with them. This I promise you. The next few months will be fulfilling and exhilarating, yet draining and disheartening—the longest year of your life, and the shortest. Expect many ups and downs and avoid becoming too discouraged. You may sometimes feel as though someone has given you a gigantic jigsaw puzzle with at least 1,000 pieces. The only problem is that you have not been given a picture of how it will look when it is put together. I hope to provide that picture.

In helping you through this year, I begin with what could be the most productive and important time period: the few weeks before the school year begins. The more time you spend preparing, the more smoothly your school year will begin. You will also find suggestions for surviving the first day, managing student behavior, getting to know your students, establishing effective parent rapport, maintaining a stimulating classroom, and more. This manual will not tell you how to teach core subjects, but you will find many ideas for enriching your classroom activities in creative and meaningful ways. Remember that, as in any other profession that deals directly with people, you cannot satisfy all expectations of all groups: administrators, parents, children, and your own family and friends. Set short-range and long-range goals for yourself and simply do the best you can. Refer to the last chapter often and pat yourself on the back every time you add a new teaching skill to your daily routine. As your students grow, learn, and change during this year, so will you.

If you are fortunate, you will find a kindred spirit in a helpful, experienced fellow staff member during your first year. I urge you to search long and hard for such a mentor. Your principal or supervisor may be able to suggest a teacher either in your school or in another nearby who might be a suitable and amiable consultant for your first year. Some school systems have started Master Teacher programs and have selected some of the finest, most dedicated educators available to help all teachers, new or veteran, do their best work. In larger school districts, there are many specialists whose sole job is to work with teachers to explain, demonstrate, and facilitate the instruction of subject matter within a particular field of expertise. If you are not getting the help you need, ask, ask, and ask again until you do.

You will probably be asked to attend several meetings and in-services for new teachers. Be watchful and follow your intuition to find other new teachers at these gatherings with whom you might strike up friendships based on common interests and needs. Nothing is quite as reassuring as knowing you are not alone in your uncertainties. But even if you discover such a soul mate, you will save valuable time and postpone the onset of gray hair by using a few of the tried and true ideas suggested in this manual.

Although it would be virtually impossible to use all the ideas and suggestions offered here during your first year, if you find only a few ideas that make your fledgling year less stressful, then I have achieved my objective.

There is a list of suggested readings at the end of each chapter. They enhance the ideas put forth in each chapter and provide much food for thought. All the resources are excellent, but an asterisk (*) appears by the ones that I feel will be most helpful to you this first year. You should be able to find these books and magazines at your professional resource library or public library. I often put books I would like to have on wish lists for family and friends.

When Dr. Haim Ginott, the noted authority on child-rearing, first started teaching, he made this inspiring observation:

> I have come to a frightening conclusion. I am the decisive element in the classroom. It is my personal approach that creates the climate. It is my daily mood that makes the weather. As a teacher, I possess tremendous power to make a child's life miserable or joyous, I can be a tool of torture or an instrument of inspiration. I can humiliate or humor, hurt or heal. In all situations it is my response that decides whether a crisis will be escalated or de-escalated, and a child humanized or de-humanized.[1]

To the new teacher, I offer my best wishes and a heartfelt welcome to a lifetime filled with the wonders of the realm of children's experiences. You may be planning to enter the classroom to teach. You may soon find, as I did, that you will stay in the classroom to learn. The challenges before you will shape your life in countless ways you have not yet even imagined.

Note

1. Dr. Haim G. Ginott. *Teacher and Child.* New York: Avon Books, 1972, p. 13.

Acknowledgments

My sincere appreciation to the many co-workers who supported my efforts to complete this project: Lisa Elder, Sherry Triantos, Maureen McCabe, Robbie Hardaway, and Nadyne Guzman for reading my initial writings and urging me to keep putting my ideas on paper. Thanks also to my artist friend, Linda Martin, who listened to my ideas and transformed them into the wonderful illustrations in this book.

I especially want to thank my daughter, Kathleen, a writer, and her husband, Scott Smith, an editor, for smoothing the rough edges. Most of all, I want to thank my husband, Larry, who always gives me the time, space, and encouragement I need and who kept Mac up, running, and glitch-free throughout the entire process.

1
Get Ready

_____

Some of the ideas in this chapter will ensure that the physical setup of your classroom is as well organized as possible before your students arrive the first day. Every classroom in an elementary school has a feel all its own. This is commonly called *classroom climate*. The climate you create will speak to everyone who enters your room and will attest to your philosophy of teaching, life, and interpersonal relationships long before you utter your first words. Following are ideas for organizing your storage areas, decorating the entrance to your classroom, preparing your desk for maximum usage, establishing reading and study areas, displaying students' work, creating a message board, and using bulletin boards.

Before creating your own unique classroom, however, you must first familiarize yourself with the school building and the school grounds as a whole. If you use this time to orient yourself—even before you meet the school staff and learn your school's particular procedures—your planning and preparation will go much more smoothly.

Touring the Building

After receiving your building and classroom assignment (Congratulations!), arrange to visit your school and acquaint yourself with your new surroundings. Tour the entire building and grounds and mentally note the location of various supply closets, restrooms, the teachers' lounge, the gymnasium, exits to the playground, computer labs, support personnel offices, special classrooms, and the music room.

Evaluating the Classroom Climate

Creating your own physical classroom atmosphere is an area in which your individuality, creativity, and personality can be expressed to the fullest. Try to gain access to your school several weeks before classes begin and spend a few quiet minutes alone, sitting in your classroom, simply looking at the raw materials with which you will work. In your room, there will probably be students' desks, your desk, a file cabinet, a couple of tables, and little else. Your imagination will be taxed as you mentally transform this bleak setting into the classroom of your dreams, but familiarizing yourself with this space is crucial.

Noting the Amenities

Measure bulletin boards. Look for other possible display areas, such as blank wall space and solid doors, and explore the possibilities for hanging things from the ceiling. Do you have a sink? Drinking fountain? Windows? (I hope you have windows!) Areas shared with other teachers or staff? Carpeted areas? Wall maps? Film screen? Bookshelves? Flag holder? Clock? Intercom? Where will children hang their coats? Where will you hang your coat?

Photographing Your Classroom

It will be difficult to remember every detail of your classroom when you leave the building, so you might want to take a few snapshots. These will be great fun to look at a few weeks down the road after you have moved in and made the room your own. Years from now, you will look back at these first photographs and recall many memories—some with a little pain, many with great joy, and most sure to bring a laugh or a smile.

Sketching a Floor Plan

Sketch a quick floor plan of your room and make notes of all the details so you can do a good deal of planning at home. Then, in your mind, begin to make this barren chamber the place you and your students will love to come to every school day. And now, the real fun begins.

Creating a Unique Classroom

Let me propose a few ways to make your classroom unique, comfortable, and inviting to primary-age children. I hope the months before you begin your first teaching assignment will not find you financially destitute; most of the suggestions I offer may require some personal investment. If an outlay of funds is absolutely impossible for you at this time, don't read the rest of this chapter until after your first payday.

Ask your principal if there is a classroom or building allowance with which you may purchase items. If no such allowance exists at your school, make a list of items you need and send a copy of the list to parents asking for donations of their discards. Fellow teachers can advise you about businesses that assist educators with special projects.

Cleaning the Cupboards

Allow yourself at least one full day devoted entirely to the cleaning and organization of storage areas. Unless you have been assigned to a brand-new school, your classroom cupboards will probably contain artifacts from the previous teacher—perhaps from several previous teachers. (Some cabinets might conceivably even reveal artifacts worthy of the Smithsonian!) By all means, empty every possible storage space. Take inventory. Put back only those items you are fairly sure you will be able to use, dispose of the rest, and then begin to make these spaces your own. Check with your principal for appropriate ways to discard the things you do not want in your room.

Many years ago I packed up a box of Dick and Jane books. Fortunately, I stored them away as curiosities. In the past few years I have resurrected them for several in-services and displays on "Reading over the Years." Educational reforms are rapidly changing the look of the curriculum in use. It is well worth saving samples of the items we use now for historical documentation.

Labeling Storage Areas

Use a label maker to designate what goes where, or use masking tape to make labels for shelving. Simply write on the tape with permanent marker. For very young prereaders, draw rebus pictures of the items instead of words, or use both to promote reading and literacy.

Countless times during a hectic day you will find your mind reeling with minor details: Where is the small red construction paper? Blue paint? Primary writing paper? Labels on the doors will cut down on time spent searching through cabinets. Keep in mind that your students should share the responsibility of keeping the classroom orderly. They should have the freedom to get the materials they need without interrupting you, and labeling promotes reading and independence as well. On the first day of class, you can plan a time to explain to children their roles in keeping their classroom orderly.

Other Labeling Ideas

In my current Chapter I Reading classroom,[1] where I instruct children from kindergarten to fourth grade, I label *everything* with small word cards. By October, my literacy-deprived students have become curious about the labels. My older students soon learn to incorporate this gratis vocabulary into their writings.

My classroom is print-rich from ceiling to floor. I use colored bookbinding tape to seal large, laminated alphabet letters in upper- and lowercase in a circle on the floor. As the kindergartners begin building sight vocabulary, these words are also taped to the floor. We play a variety of games in which the children move around the circle, stop, and practice usage of their knowledge of each letter or word. "Spin the Bottle" is one of their favorites. Tossing bean bags to each letter, then naming the letter and a word that begins with that letter is good practice. These letters last for one year, are taken up in June, and are replaced again the following fall.

In the area where the children line up to exit my room, the numbers 1 to 20, along with a corresponding number of dots, are laminated on a variety of colored construction papers that are taped to the floor. All of my students enjoy the orderliness this brings to dismissal as I say, "John, you may line up on number nine," or "Mary, today you may line up on pink." Kindergartners and first-graders may be asked to check their number with the dots. In the corner of each number square is the ordinal—first, second, third—as well as the cardinal number—one, two, three. I use every minute of my brief time with these children to pack in literacy in a fun yet relevant way.

Decorating the Entrance to Your Room

Decorating the entrance to your classroom is a delightful way to welcome everyone who crosses your threshold. Your doorway can be used to celebrate holidays, announce special learning activities, set a mood, suggest an inner environment, or highlight a season of the year. One-inch-thick plastic foam cutouts of giant valentine candy hearts, shamrocks, Easter eggs, gaily wrapped gifts, jack-o-lanterns, oversized insects, flowers, birds, snowmen, and Christmas trees are eye-catching holiday objects that can be used perennially. (Styrofoam must be spray-painted with paint created just for this purpose. Standard spray paints will dissolve the Styrofoam, so check the label before using.) A standard doorway can be surrounded by butcher paper cut in the shape of a tree, cave, cloud, teepee, log cabin (see fig. 1.1), castle, spaceship, or just about any object suggestive of areas of interest in your classroom.

At the beginning of the year, framed self-portraits of students surrounding the doorway attest to the sense of community experienced within. One idea for such portraits is to give the children dessert-size paper plates and yarn the color of their hair. The children will not disappoint you. Keep a few inexpensive hand mirrors around so the children can really look at themselves as they add details. Suggest that they look for missing teeth, freckles, ear shapes, and other characteristics that make them unique and special.

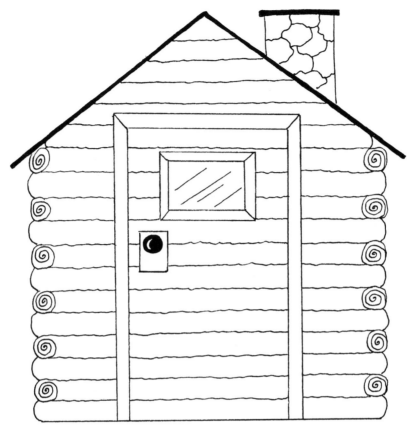

Fig. 1.1. Use decorated butcher paper to create a "log cabin" around your doorway.

Making the Most of Your Desk

Every teacher has a personal banner that says more about him or her than any résumé could ever incorporate: the classroom desk. Here are a few tips to make the most of this important classroom fixture.

The Desktop

Your desktop can be a very personal statement of your feelings about teaching, your family and friends, and your philosophy of life in general. It is your home base and should reflect your priorities and personality. And just like home plate, you don't score any points if you don't leave it and hustle around the other bases.

Most teachers' desks are made of metal and consist of five or six drawers, a broad work surface, one or two pullout writing surfaces, and a large knee-hole space. A few rare schools have salvaged or still use traditional oak desks—they are beautiful and functional, but you may find that they take their toll on stockings and clothing if you don't take the time to sand the edges of the kneeholes.

I like to keep my desk in an out-of-the-way place and share it with my students. Years ago I made a one-time investment and had a piece of beveled plate glass cut to desktop measurements. Over the years, I have placed beneath this glass many photographs and documents, creating a current collage of important events and the people related to them. Every year one picture is the same: an old, *old* photo of my own second-grade class. I challenge my children to find me in the picture. (Oddly enough, my students almost always choose a little girl third from the right in the back row and insist that it must be me. It's not! That's Donna Nelson. I'm fifth from the left in the front row.) I leave plenty of space around the edges each fall and soon the border is filled with much-used school phone numbers, new recipes for classroom projects, names of visitors to our class, unique greeting cards, catchy bumper stickers, poignant messages from students, and many other little items that slip easily under the edge of the glass. In this way, I give my students glimpses of my personal life that often serve as springboards for intimate conversations. It is just one more easy way to bond with your students. My desktop is user friendly, and I sometimes take a few seconds to just sit at the desk and center myself when I am feeling frustrated or tired.

The sides of a metal desk are ideal places for children to display papers they want to share with the class. You might want to use one end for a message board. I keep a basket on my desktop filled with small magnets for this purpose; you can also use cellophane tape. The children are free to put up anything they wish.

The Drawers

One drawer is used for daily record-keeping documents such as lunch money envelopes, attendance books, grade books, field trip collection envelopes, and any other frequently updated paperwork. Another drawer is used for spare parts, such as chalk, rulers, pencils, erasers, paper clips, staples, rubber bands, and other small tools of the trade. The largest drawer is used for storing curriculum guides, district policy manuals, parent handbooks, building policies, teachers' meeting folders, and packets to be given to new students and their families. Make up a few extra packets of all information, handouts, permission slips, parent handbooks, and supply lists so that welcoming a new child goes as smoothly as possible.

Another drawer is designated as the classroom Lost and Found Department. This drawer reinforces individual and class responsibility and saves many valuable minutes each day. I ask that the night custodian put any objects he or she finds, including pencils and crayons, into this drawer. When students find they don't have needed supplies, they may borrow or reclaim items from this drawer until they can bring more of their own. I never discard pencil or crayon nubbins of more than an inch and a half long. Using short pencils intrinsically motivates children to get better ones from home, and you don't have to say a word.

Some teachers create an order form for supplies that children need to replenish from home on a regular basis, such as pencils, crayons, and markers. All you need to do is fill in the child's name and date, check the items needed, and send home as necessary. Compile a master of your class list on grid paper and make several photocopies. These will be useful for a variety of tasks. You can easily keep track of homework assignments, field trip permissions, and grade records for different projects, as well as who has returned various forms to be sent to the office, or what classroom books or center packets have been taken home. You can also send a class list home to parents to familiarize them with the names of the other students in your class. Young children love to talk about their school friends, and parents often don't know the names of all the students in their child's class. Before Valentine's Day I always send home this list with each child. You will find numerous other uses for these handy rosters.

The center kneehole drawer is the shallowest and is my only personal drawer for supplies. Stored here are the stationery and notepads on which I write letters and memos to parents and children. Kept here also are adhesive bandages to lavish on children's small sores. A new item, added to this drawer a couple of years ago because of the rising incidence of AIDS, is a pair of green medical gloves to be used whenever handling a child who has incurred an injury resulting in bleeding. Wearing these gloves at such times is a policy recently adopted by many schools. If you are given no literature regarding an AIDS policy, ask your principal, school secretary, or school nurse how to attend to such situations. Unfortunately, I have donned these gloves many times in the past couple of years.

The last drawer is the most fun for us all. Over the years, you will accumulate the oddest assortment of junk and may already have started this peculiar teacher habit. In our junk drawer you can find more than 200 "leftover" items, from A to Z! I don't know exactly what this drawer is for, except that it's really necessary and it's really important for us to have it there. I know that nothing is ever taken from it and not returned. I know that I am not the only one who adds to it, but I never see who else does. I know that we all need a little time to sit at a big desk and just look at *stuff*.

The Pullouts

The desk's two pullout writing surfaces can be in constant use. On one you might tape the school's calendar for the year. On the other you might tape a class list with student phone numbers, so it is handy and can be updated as necessary. A child can call the class roll from this list in the morning while you document the absences. Children love to sit at the big desk and share classroom management duties. It is one more way to give them ownership of their school experience.

Encourage the children to use these pullouts in other ways. They make an excellent alternative place to do writing or math assignments when a child needs or wants to be away from classmates. Children who have a difficult time sitting to complete assignments find the pullouts the perfect height for standing while writing. Being able to sit for long periods of time to complete a task is simply beyond some students' abilities, as you will soon discover. Avoid behavior problems with some children by allowing them the choice to stand up and do their work either at their own desks or at yours. It's a simple bit of advice, but it works.

You can also use the pullouts as a convenient and semiprivate place to do conferencing and individual assessments. There is hardly a minute in the day when the pullouts are not in use by some member of our class.

The Kneehole

The kneehole is the ultimate place for a child to push in a couple of floor cushions and read, study, talk to himself or herself, hum, or just be alone. I have even found a student sound asleep under my desk on occasion. There will be moments when you wish you could fit in there, too!

Personal Items on Your Desktop

Across the back of the desktop, I keep a row of my most used resource books, textbook manuals, and four reference books—a regular dictionary, a Spanish/English dictionary, a thesaurus, and a rhyming dictionary. When your finances allow, purchase a set of decorative bookends. Perhaps you could put these on a wish list for your birthday or other holiday. Showing off your books in a way that demonstrates how much you value them is just another way to model the significance of a good education. In my collection are three of my childhood storybooks preserved from the World War II era, when children's books were rare and precious. I have had to laminate them to protect them from the hands of many, many curious children. For some students, your classroom may be the only place where they see an adult taking education seriously. Use every opportunity to set a good example.

I think it is lovely to keep a live plant or two on the desktop. Philodendrons and pothos do especially well under artificial lighting and take a reasonable amount of neglect in stride.

Other Storage Ideas

Your day will run more smoothly if each child has a designated cubbyhole for papers to be taken home. At dismissal time, students simply gather any stored items and put them in their backpacks or totes. If your classroom has no built-in cubbies, tiered cardboard shoe-storage boxes from the discount department store are more than adequate and can be a colorful addition to your decor. A pyramid of oatmeal boxes, covered with adhesive-backed paper and hot-glued in place, is another inexpensive alternative. Office supply stores also carry inexpensive, open-faced cabinets that are ideal for providing multiple storage areas. With any such system, it is easy to quickly determine which students are not taking their things home. At the end of the day make a visit to the cubbies a part of the classroom routine.

File Cabinets

There will probably be a two- or four-drawer file cabinet in your room. In no time you will have filled every available space, but while you still have room, make file folders for each student and put them in the bottom drawer. Keep all confidential information in these folders, such as past records from other schools, registration forms, and notes to and from parents, Social Services, health agencies, and so on.

◆ Portfolios

It is wise to keep periodic samples of each child's work in all subject areas for progress monitoring, reporting to parents, district accountability, and, most importantly, for the children themselves so that they can follow their own improvement. The latest terminology for this type of data collecting is called *building a portfolio*. I keep most of my students' records in these files, and the children are free to look into their own at any time. Most students take the time and the responsibility to keep their files organized and neat. The content of the portfolios will reflect your instructional goals, as well as each child's individual choices for preservation. Papers and projects that may seem insignificant to you may be very important to the child, and it is ultimately that child's portfolio. A copy of the student's current report card is also kept here. Many districts have, or soon will have, portfolios to demonstrate student proficiency.

◆ Other Folders

Another file drawer is used to keep teaching materials organized by subject or unit of study. You can now purchase colorful filing dividers and folders at office supply stores, and these can make a tedious job much more interesting.

Your school's art supply room will also have 9-x-12-inch construction paper. Folded in half, this paper makes handy and colorful folders, although they are not durable. Encourage children to decorate their folders. Some students like to collect stickers on the back because they will be taking their folders home at the end of the school year. Be sure to make copies of any papers you want to keep in their permanent portfolios.

◆ Using Your File Cabinet As a Teaching Tool

The outer surfaces of the file cabinet present more areas on which you may display children's work or create learning centers. By providing magnets with clips or magnetic plastic strips, children can put up whatever they wish. One side can be a photo gallery or message board. You might also paint one side with spray "chalkboard," available at most hardware stores. Children love to write on the chalkboard, and this makes one available to them at all times. On another surface, glue a large piece of felt and provide felt numbers, letters, story figures, and scenic cutouts.

The top of the file cabinet is a safe but visible surface for showing off breakables and delicate items for "touching with eyes only." I often bring in a few of my personal treasures to place there after I've shared them with the class. When parents know you have a safe display area, they will let their children bring in family treasures.

Creating Reading and Study Areas

Think of unique ways to encourage reading by using all extra spaces in your classroom for individual or small-group comfort zones. In my classroom, there is a storage cabinet three feet high by five feet long located next to a window. I bought a four-inch-thick piece of foam rubber pad, covered it with an old flannel sheet, and placed it on top of this cabinet, along with a nice soft pillow. It is now the reading couch, and throughout the day is in constant use by some avid, snuggled-up, little scholar. I have also let children with an occasional headache or stomach ache take a break there until I can determine whether they really need to go home for the day. Usually, a little time on the couch and some T.L.C. are all that are needed.

Two students fit easily into my resale-store, overstuffed rocking chair for shared reading. One year an artistic mom brought in a discarded cardboard refrigerator shipping box. She turned it on its side and, with a little window cutting and the application of some brightly colored paints, created a wonderful native hut to enhance our study of the jungle. Beanbag chairs are comfortable, portable, and provide safe seating alternatives for students, particularly physically challenged ones.

Creating Comfort Zones

The most useful purchases I have ever made are an overstuffed rocking chair, a small end table, a living room table lamp, and a 7-x-10-foot oval braided rug. If you prefer a more portable floor seating arrangement, one that can virtually be put away when not in use, ask a carpet dealer to save outdated rug samples for you. These little rectangles of carpeting are perfect for providing each child with his or her own little floor tuffet. The carpet samples can be put in a cozy circle or whatever arrangement suits the activity of the moment. My entire collection of furnishings totaled $70 at Goodwill and Salvation Army resale shops. You could probably do even better at garage sales. Perhaps relatives or friends might loan or give you used furniture.

These items are the central focus of our classroom. They speak of home, comfort, warmth, and our feelings about learning and teaching. We spend more valuable hours each day in the area created by these few relics than we do at our desks.

Other Items for the Classroom

Other salvage collectibles to watch for over the years are children's rockers or chairs; a child's antique wooden school desk (the more initials carved in, the better the stories you can concoct about its past); sturdy beanbag chairs; a rolling kitchen storage basket stack; additional bookshelves; small display cases; aquaria and small cages (if you are animal-oriented); an upholstered rolling desk chair (no back) to use at the reading table; an easel chalkboard; a wooden clothes drying rack for displaying books or artwork; a wooden dropleaf kitchen table to be used for an art center; coffee tables (indispensable for work that requires kneeling); picture frames; unusual bookends; an old podium cut down so that it is child-size; small and large throw pillows; magazine racks; and a tall stool. The tall stool is the throne from which my children do show-and-tell, read their best works, talk to the class, give reports, show their works of art, or perform. If your budget is really tight, ask children to bring in some items—with parental permission, of course. Yes, our classroom has been likened to a sanitary landfill, but it is also full of variety, color, and choices.

Be sure to keep every receipt for the expenditures you make each year, whether for pens and pencils, books, used furniture, or anything else you purchase to use for your students. Consult your tax advisor, as many items are deductible and may save you some money next April 15.

Shoe Bags

One of the handiest items you can get at a wholesale shopping mart is a multipocketed shoe bag. I keep one attached to the chalk rail behind me at our conference or reading table. Use it to hold pencils, erasers, colored markers, scissors, staplers, hole punches, brads, paper clips, rulers, flashcards, note paper, and stickers. (Yes, I give stickers now and then. Tape a sheet of paper or large index card to each child's desk so that he or she can collect stickers there and take them home periodically.)

The Treasure Box

A doll's clothing trunk or decorated cardboard box with a lid makes an ideal treasure box. I fill mine with inexpensive items such as balloons, plastic costume jewelry, children's card games, small rubber balls, toy cars and trucks, and many other items I discover in discount stores. My students earn a trip to the treasure box when they have accumulated 10 stars, stickers, or other symbols awarded for a day's appropriate behavior. I keep track of the stars or stickers on index cards at the reading table. This is a simple and effective behavior management tool that has always been popular with my students.

Jars, Baskets, and Containers

Start saving small containers. You have probably received little baskets of soap or notepaper, decorative tins, colorful jars, candy boxes with little compartments, berry baskets, or even plastic glasses, and have them in the back of a cabinet or closet. Now you can use them *all*. Keep these containers filled with the various items children may need throughout the day. When students need a paper clip, brad, scissors, or whatever you decide to put out for their use, they soon associate their needs with the design of the container that holds that item. You and the children are saved a great deal of time from the eternal hunt. If you enlist a student to be supply master, he or she can see to it that items are replenished from the drawer in your desk whenever necessary. Encourage children to bring odds-and-ends containers of their own to keep in or on their desks. All of these ideas build independence, responsibility, and ownership for your students.

Attendance and Lunch Count Charts

For simple attendance and lunch counts, create a chart made with library book pockets, one for each child. You can probably get these from the school librarian. In the morning, each child puts a colored strip of paper in his or her chart pocket to indicate hot lunch (red) or brown-bag lunch from home (yellow). A quick glance at the chart gives you a lunch tally and also signals children who are absent.

Message Boards

The message board has many purposes. It fosters written communication between you and your children and provides a forum where students can exchange messages with each other. It increases children's reading, writing, and spelling skills and reduces the number of verbal interruptions. It gives every class member the power of the written word.

Appropriate items for the message board are notes voicing problems, needs, wants, questions, words of encouragement, constructive criticism, feelings, announcements, current events, reminders, suggestions, ideas, worries, invitations, successes, compliments, and losses. Used in this way, the message board is much like the classified section of the newspaper (and sometimes like the personal section).

Initially, children look forward to checking the board frequently for folded messages to them personally or open messages for the entire class, written and posted by you. As writing skills increase and the comfort level rises, students will begin to add their own notes to the board.

Many messages will require written responses from you and will be wonderful opportunities to establish personal dialogues with your students. Other items will provide topics for lively class discussions. By using the message board, children frequently resolve peer conflicts without having verbal confrontations.

Other items that add variety and interest to the board are cartoons, jokes, riddles, and small drawings and pictures. Rebus messages are helpful in first grade when writing skills are beginning to emerge. Prohibit the use of the board for tattling and hurtful purposes—the poison pen is not allowed, and all messages must be signed. Everyone is responsible for removing their own items when they are no longer current.

The message board can occupy a variety of locations. A designated section of existing bulletin board easily reached by all class members is ideal. The front of your metal desk works well if you provide small magnets to secure the items to be posted. Free-standing feltboards can serve as portable message boards, as can the small cork bulletin boards found at discount department stores. A unique space-saving idea is to obtain a cardboard tube from a carpet roll, place it upright in a corner of the room, and use it in the same manner as college students use a kiosk.

(A few paper fronds makes mine look like a palm tree [see fig. 1.2]. During the winter holidays, it is a sugar-plum tree, wrapped in red and white candy stripes with giant Styrofoam lollipops sticking out of the top.)

Fig. 1.2. A kiosk-style message board.

Bulletin Boards

There is an abundance of books on the subject of creating bulletin boards. Most contain wonderful ideas, but keep in mind that the classroom is to be shared. Give your students ownership by allowing them to co-plan and execute bulletin boards with you. See the Resources section at the end of this chapter for a few of the more creative bulletin board books. If I had my way, teacher supply stores would not stock any preprinted bulletin board items other than border materials. With few exceptions, prefab bulletin boards are a poor substitute for student/teacher designed displays.

Imposing my well-designed, esthetically correct bulletin boards into my students' learning environment is probably as meaningful for them as if I gave an interior decorator a free hand to design and decorate my home office for me. For the past few years I have experimented with how much my students really notice in the classroom, including the bulletin boards. There is no question that they are much more aware of and learn more from displays of information in which they have been directly involved.

Displaying 25 copies of the same worksheet as a "good work" bulletin board denies the creativity of children and their teacher. Twenty-five individual versions of Pippi Longstockings, Mrs. Piggle Wiggle, Charlotte, or self-portraits would certainly be more fun and meaningful.

Your school will probably have large rolls of butcher paper in a variety of colors for covering the boards. If not, find a party supply store and let your imagination be your guide as you choose affordable background materials from the many choices of paper and plastic table coverings now available. Burlap also works well and lasts for years. Have your children make colorful borders by simply tracing their hands or feet and cutting out the shapes. Staple the cutouts around the perimeter of your boards and you will have one of the most unique and personal bulletin boards in your school.

On one board, you might put a simple background of blue sky, brown rolling hills or mountains, and a green, grassy foreground. Invite your students to do the rest. You will be amazed at their enthusiasm and ingenuity in finishing the project.

One year I gave each of my students a paper lunch sack and all the materials, including cotton stuffing and yarn, to create their own heads for a bulletin board titled "Mount Classmore." Large objects like these can be anchored to the bulletin board with corsage pins from an arts and crafts store. I showed them pictures of Mount Rushmore and we did a mini-unit on presidents and an additional art activity on creating busts from clay. The bulletin board was hilarious and a big hit on Back-to-School Night.

Create a large school bus, city bus, covered wagon, hot-air balloon, blimp, ocean liner, sailboat, train, or airplane out of butcher paper. Incorporate enough windows or portholes so that you and every child can display a self-portrait.

Give everyone a circle of white paper the size of a quart jar lid. Have the children create self-portraits using crayons, markers, and bits of colored yarn or construction paper for hair. As with many activities, be sure to include yourself and model by creating your own self-portrait first. Allow the children to put their faces in the window of their choice. This bulletin board can be a motivational activity for a unit on transportation or geography.

When You Have No Windows

Classrooms with no windows are, for me, aberrations to be dealt with immediately. The windowless school was designed to reduce heating bills, construction costs, and vandalism. They also reduce exposure to sunshine, cloud formations, the flight of birds, the sounds of passersby, the wind in the trees, awareness of the time of day, ventilation and a breath of fresh air, and current weather conditions, and deprive most of us of the chance to daydream. Here is one way to foil the system, albeit a poor substitute for the real thing. Construct a mock windowframe from strips of Styrofoam or heavy cardboard, any size you like. Make paper or fabric curtains to tie back at the sides. Have the children design and paint a scene they wish they could see from their classroom and mount it behind your new "window." Change the scene periodically, perhaps to correspond with the changing seasons or to match a topic of current study in your class. In the fall, my students create a row of deserted and dilapidated mansions and leafless trees, visible through the panes of our pretend window. Even if you do have windows, a bulletin board could be turned into one to accommodate these decorating ideas.

The Ceiling

The space over your head has many useful possibilities too. If there are not already eyescrews in the walls near the ceiling to put up twine from one end of the room to the other, ask your principal if such an arrangement is possible. If so, ask the custodian to put up a few for you immediately. Fire safety regulations must be observed, so be sure the strings will not come within a foot of lighting or alarm systems. Hanging anything from ceiling tiles or light fixtures is usually prohibited.

Throughout the coming year you will find many opportunities to use this overhead hanging space. Half-opened paper clips or clothespins will probably be all the fasteners you will need. Using a hole punch, you can display exemplary papers done by the children, sight words, numbers, works of art, paper T-shirts, and any manner of lightweight objects. Kindergartners and first-graders like to make caterpillars to hang from the strings. Each child is given 28 circles of different colors of construction paper. The first circle is the head, the last circle is a name tag, and the letters of the alphabet are put on the remaining circles. Then they are connected to each other with staples or brads. I give the students little green feet to glue to each circle and then we suspend the finished caterpillars overhead.

When working on a particular unit of study, children can create wonderful stuffed objects to enhance their environment. When we study the ocean, each child chooses to "become" one of the denizens of the deep. They create their creatures by making duplicate, oversized replicas of their animals out of butcher paper, stuffing them with scrap paper, stapling the two pieces together, and hanging them from the ceiling twine. Thinly cut crêpe-paper streamers hung between each of the animals recreates an undersea environment right in our room.

We have created other environments using the air space in our room, too; the forest, the desert, the farm, mountains, the circus, outer space, a Native American village, and the jungle. We decorate our classroom windows and doors so that our entire classroom is transformed into another time or place. Our weekly spelling lists, story, math, social studies, science, centers, nutrition, enriched reading, drama, and music activities all reflect the central theme of our studies. These environments remain intact for most of the year.

Summary

The classroom climate you create for your students will speak to them before you ever say a single word. Parents, children, fellow staff members, and your principal will all note that you are well prepared and ready to begin a new school year. Of course the room will undergo changes during the year, as its uses and the children's input demand, but your initial preparation and personalization set the tone right from the start. "Nest" in your classroom well before the first day with students, and your comfort level will rise to ease you through the first few hectic days. Children love walking into a room that says, "Welcome. I've been waiting for you!"

Notes

1. Chapter I is a federally funded program in place under that title in every state in the United States. It is a legally funded program and recognized in many schools throughout the country. It used to be called Title I.

Resources

(Note: The asterisk [*] denotes titles I believe are most helpful to first year teachers.)

Andrews, Rebecca S., and Lynn B. Coble. *Bulletin Boards for Busy Teachers*. Greensboro, N.C.: Education Center, 1992.

*Canoles, Marian L. *The Creative Copycat*. Littleton, Colo.: Libraries Unlimited, 1982.

Christensen, Ann, and Lee Green. *Trash to Treasures: An Idea Book for Classroom and Media Center Materials*. Littleton, Colo.: Libraries Unlimited, 1982.

Holt, John. *What Do I Do Monday?* New York: Stratford Press, 1970.

*Loughlin, Catherine E., and Mavis D. Martin. *Supporting Literacy: Developing Effective Learning Environments*. New York: Teachers College Press, 1987.

Mallett, Jerry J. *Reading Bulletin Boards and Displays.* West Nyack, N.Y.: Center for Applied Research in Education, 1988.

*Spizman, Robyn. *All Aboard with Bulletin Boards.* Carthage, Ill.: Good Apple, 1983.

2
Get Set

By now, I hope you have been able to use and investigate your classroom, so that you can plan and actually begin to prepare it well before children arrive for that momentous first day. Now is the time, as the day draws ever closer, to get to know your school's staff and procedures; prepare yourself for the year to come; organize your lesson plans; and contact your students and their families for the first time.

Everyone with whom you work, be it school staff, children, parents, or others in the community, will have an effect on what you do in your classroom and how you do it. Of course, your school's requirements, procedures, and guidelines will also influence your classroom management and presentation, so it is helpful to prepare your classroom and lessons with a thorough knowledge of those requirements.

Meet School Personnel

The Principal

One of the most important people in your life this year will be your school principal. Principals are trained to acquire skills and know resources to help new teachers along the way. Your success this year is therefore also the principal's success, and your growth and adjustment to a new career is a challenge for your principal as well, so work together closely throughout the coming months. Communicate your apprehensions as well as your strengths and ask for guidance whenever you need it. Admit your shortcomings and ask for the principal's opinions and advice. Share your students' achievements freely and often. Keep your principal informed of upcoming events and celebrations in your classroom and your life.

Take the time to thoroughly understand what is expected of you. Strict adherence to the time lines involved in the evaluation of a new teacher is crucial. You are being asked to prove your professional abilities these first months. Always ask for assistance with any procedures you don't completely understand. Talk to the other teachers in your building about their experiences with assessment and ask for their advice.

If struggles arise between you and parents or co-workers, use your best people skills to solve these problems yourself in a professional manner. If you are unable to resolve your differences, seek the counsel of your principal, but avoid going to your principal with petty problems, and always keep your conflicts confidential. Discuss them only with the persons directly involved. New teachers, fairly or unfairly, are being judged this first year by their co-workers, parents, and sometimes even their students. You will gain respect and trust by not gossiping about other staff members and families in your school. Blow off steam with a relative or friend outside of school, but always protect the privacy of those involved.

Every principal has opinions about the characteristics that are most important in a teacher. You would be wise to know what the expectations are in your building. When setting your goals for this year with your principal, be open and honest about any feelings of inadequacy. Your principal will want to help you with an ongoing professional growth plan and can be your closest ally when difficulties arise. You are going to learn much more than you teach in the next few months. Be open to suggestions and at least give them a try. But don't stifle your enthusiasm and creativity. You are bringing with you to our profession a breath of fresh air, and there are some old dogs out here eager to learn your new tricks.

Ask your principal for a copy of a staff roster and memorize the names and positions of each co-worker before the first day of school. You may even be able to get a staff photo from the previous year, which would be even more helpful. If you will have a teammate, try to arrange to have coffee or lunch together several days before school starts. A co-worker may be able to answer most of your questions and give helpful suggestions for getting off on the right foot. Within most schools, close friendships build, endure, and will sustain and enrich your life through the years ahead. If you don't have a teammate or grade-level partner, your principal may be able to suggest someone on staff who could be a consultant for you during these first few weeks. Perhaps you will find someone at a nearby school.

The School Secretary

The school secretary may well be the most important co-worker in the building, often providing the first contact, whether it is on the telephone or at the front desk, that teachers, parents, the public, and children have with the school. In fact, secretaries are often called office managers, because that is truly what they are. Little goes on in a school that the secretary is not involved in. The job description is multifaceted and the skills required are varied. A talented school secretary is invaluable and is usually underrated and overworked by the many people he or she interacts with each hour of the day. Duties range from first aid for students to highly technical computer data input. The secretary rarely finds an uninterrupted five-minute time period to perform her clerical duties.

Your secretary will appreciate it greatly if you are able to plan your day well enough not to ask him or her to stop work to help you find a few sheets of paper or other office supplies during school hours. Arrive early enough each day to attend to your classroom needs prior to the children's arrival. Ask your friends and relatives to call you at school only in emergencies. As with all other school support persons, ask what you can do to make their jobs easier and always acknowledge their kindnesses to you in some way. I have a little stash of comical pencils that I give out, along with a little thank-you note, when the secretary or someone else has gone out of the way to help me. These little extras are always appreciated and have helped me establish better rapport with co-workers. A little bouquet and a nice card on Secretary's Day and birthdays are appropriate, too.

The Library Technician

At the beginning of the year, ask your media technician or school librarian for a few minutes to help familiarize you with the resources available in your building. Your librarian will be able to help you with countless activities, from putting together social studies units to enriching your curriculum for gifted-and-talented students. Also ask to see the school's collection of books and manuals for your own professional growth.

Become especially familiar with the media center. Take a few minutes to familiarize yourself with the card catalog and the location of student books and resources for teachers. Catalogs of audiovisual materials will be available in your school system. Perhaps you can take some of these home to study for a few days.

The Custodian

The people who care for the physical plant of your school may be called *custodians* or *building managers*; they are no longer called *janitors*. But whatever their title, they are there to keep the building clean and in good running order and are very important members of the school team who deserve your respect and consideration. Learn their names quickly and openly ask what your custodial duties are. Ask them what you can do to make their jobs easier. In our building, students must pick up all floor trash and place their chairs on their desks before leaving each day. If you want items on the chalkboard left for the next day, you may have to write "SAVE" nearby. Find out what tasks they will perform in your room each day and ask about special services: how to have stomach spills cleaned up, what protection you must give floors before a messy art project, how classroom plants and pets can be cared for over long weekends, who is responsible for closing windows and blinds, or anything that you feel falls in this realm.

During my first month of teaching, I assumed (*never* assume anything—ask!) that the custodian would lock all the windows at night. After a terribly hot September day in Illinois, I unthinkingly left one of my windows open and went home for the night. The building was vandalized that evening. I quickly learned to ask a lot of questions.

I bring our custodian a fresh pastry about once a month with a thank-you note for past favors. Mr. Lucero has taken care of my animals for me for the past 12 years when I could not get to school due to snowstorms or illness. How nice it is to know I have someone who cares about my creatures as much as I do. I consider him one of my best friends at school. I hope you will be as fortunate with your custodian as I have been with mine.

Other Classroom and Building Assistants

Your staff will probably include a variety of aides and assistants to help with clerical duties, special-education and bilingual students, and lunchroom and playground duties. You may occasionally be required to attend special meetings, such as student staffings and child studies, during the school day, and one of the assistants may cover your class for you during your absence. These assistants perform a variety of tasks for very little or no pay. With budget crunches, aides are being cut, and those left are working harder than ever. They have my utmost respect for their dedication and versatility. Ask your principal what each assistant's responsibilities are so that you commit no faux pas by asking them to help with inappropriate tasks. We have a special day each year to honor these hard workers. Acknowledge their efforts with a little note or gift whenever appropriate. They can help you out in tight situations when no one else can.

Other Resources in the Community

Central Resource Centers

Many larger districts have a central professional learning center filled with materials for your use, and smaller districts often consolidate their resources at some central location. Be sure to find out where this facility is located and learn the procedures for its use. My district's resource center has curriculum-related statuary, dioramas, miniature representations of Native American dwellings, artifact kits, and thousands of books and supplementary teaching materials for unlimited use. Our central resource technician is very knowledgeable and is always available and eager to help us enhance our classroom projects. Find out who your resource people are and don't hesitate to ask for guidance.

Public Library

If you have relocated to a new community, spend a little time at the public library to see what materials are available for your use. You should be able to check out multiple copies of children's books for social studies, science, and reading enrichment. Many libraries have a very good selection of educational videos for use by classroom teachers. The reference librarian is an invaluable resource. In many states you may apply for a statewide library card that gives you access to every library in the state, including those at colleges and universities. Ask for this card at your public library.

Learning the Ropes

Ask for your teachers' guides, copies of students' textbooks, a staff and student handbook, parent handbook, district curriculum, and philosophy and goal statement. Spend a few evenings familiarizing yourself with all of this information before the more pressing demands of lesson planning and grading papers are upon you.

You will be returning to these sources frequently throughout the year for particulars, but it is helpful to have a basic overview in the back of your mind. Most districts have a basic curriculum that you must use for the instruction of core subjects. There may also be a schedule of the number of minutes you must spend weekly on each subject.

Checklist of Things to Find Out About Your School

For your peace of mind and convenience, I propose seeking the answers to these questions a couple of weeks before school begins:

What time is the building opened? Closed?

May I work in my room on weekends? How do I get into the building? How do I disconnect the alarm system?

What do I do if I have to be absent? Who do I call? When?

Where are the art supplies kept? Do I have to account for materials used?

Am I allowed to use the photocopier? Who can show me how?

How do I order audio/video equipment? Where do I get forms? How far in advance?

What materials are available in the school library? How do I check them out?

How do I print worksheets? Are there any rules or limitations?

What duties do I have? Procedures?

Where and when may I use the telephone for personal business?

What do I do about a sick child? Do I need to fill out any forms?

How do I order films, filmstrips, study prints, etc.?

What are the library checkout procedures?

What are my custodial responsibilities? With what chores may I expect help?

Where are extra textbooks and workbooks stored?

How do I report lunch money?

Where and when are staff meetings held?

What after-hours obligations will I have? On what committees may I serve?

Is there a building floor plan I may have?

What security is provided for personal items? Do I have keys for my room, desk, file cabinet?

May I use hot plates, burners, and/or crock pots in the classroom?

Where are warehouse and audiovisual catalogs stored?

What are the field trip procedures?

Do I have access to any funds for purchasing items for my classroom?

Which of these are supplied for me and where do I find them?

stapler	staple remover	rubber bands
staples	yardstick	rubber gloves
tape dispenser	rulers	bandages
pens	crayons	tissue
chalk	board erasers	hand soap
scissors	paper clips	cleanser
markers	brads	sink sponges
pencils	thumbtacks	erasers

In some schools, the principal assembles a tote tray or box for every staff member, filling it with most of the items needed for their class assignment. This saves a lot of wear and tear on everyone.

Dressing for the Job

Dress modes and codes are strictly local and personalized even from school to school within one district. Primary teachers do very little sitting, and when they do, they usually sit in the same "munchkin" chairs as their students so they can maintain maximum eye contact. They do a great deal of bending over students working at short desks or tables, so, unless you are an adept stooper, miniskirts and tight trousers are out. My one suggestion is that your clothing be machine-washable, as little people will frequently share messes with you.

Taking Care of Your Feet

There are still a few older schools where architects had the foresight and raw resources to build classrooms with wood floors. Most schools are now built over concrete slabs and, even if carpeted, these floors will soon take their toll on your back, legs, and feet. Find shoes that will be comfortable for the long haul. You are in for a surprise when you see how much walking you will do each day. Keep a pair of ballet-type slippers in your desk or closet and slip into them whenever your feet start to complain. Encourage your students to kick off their shoes once in awhile. There's nothing wrong with being comfortable in a learning environment.

Unless you have worn them on a daily basis for years and have hamstrings three inches shorter than most ladies, high heels and teaching are a painful combination. Sitting at furniture designed for little people requires acrobatic positioning on your part and high heels aren't going to help. The better your eye contact with your students, the more effective your teaching will be, so try to get used to sitting on a low chair.

Taking Care of Yourself

The old maxim, "Early to bed and early to rise, makes a man healthy, wealthy and wise," are words worth heeding for at least the first few months of teaching. Most teachers spend far more than the seven or eight hours per day negotiated in a contract on their varied professional duties. There simply is no way to accomplish all of the tedious tasks required of you in so little time.

Some people are "owls" and do their best work in the late evening hours. They can afford the luxury of arriving at school half an hour before their students. Owls do their best thinking and planning after a few cups of coffee have cleared the cobwebs. They are the burners of the midnight oil and are still working when the "larks" are fast asleep.

The larks arise at dawn or sooner and arrive at school bright and early, perhaps an hour, or even two, before the children do. Their energy level is highest before noon and dwindles as the day goes on. Staying after the children have gone home, to prepare for the next day's activities, is usually unproductive for a lark.

It's fun to visit the teacher's lounge about 15 minutes before the first bell rings and do an observational inventory of the larks and owls on your staff. By the second semester, you'll have them all pegged. Thank goodness we are not all on the same energy schedule—we need to hold each other up every so often.

You probably already know which type you are and will soon know which schedule will work best for you. But be assured that your new job will not begin when the children walk through the classroom door, nor will it end when they leave in the afternoon. Never again will you cherish sleep as much as during these first few months of school. Getting enough rest is crucial to your success this first year. You'll pay the price in patience, creativity, and stamina if you burn your candle at both ends. Be good to yourself and your students by getting the amount of sleep you know you need. And don't forget to take the time you need for a little recreational exercise each day, even if it is just to walk a few blocks in the afternoon or evening. Your nervous system and muscles will thank you. A few minutes of regular exercise will help burn off tension and facilitate a restful sleep. These next few weeks may well be the most stressful of your life. Please be good to yourself.

Lesson Plan Book

Your lesson plan book will become an acquired appendage, somewhat like a cast on a broken limb. It holds everything together and is a necessary evil to a well-ordered classroom. Like your desk, it can be mundane and utilitarian or highly personalized and dynamic. I will describe my lesson plan book and then you can decide what will work best for you.

Noting Special Days

Every summer, one of my quests as I vacation and do some leisure shopping, is to keep an eye out for unusual and colorful stickers and greeting cards. In August, I buy a brand-new set of markers, both fine line and broad tip, in the brightest colors I can find. When I have a couple of hours to play, I decorate my lesson plan book by tracing over all of the vertical and horizontal line segments with contrasting colors, entering all of the dates, noting holidays, teacher work days, vacation periods, and adding stickers—some seasonal and some that are just pure whimsy—on each page. I often put a greeting-card picture or message of particular interest to me on the cover. My students enjoy my lesson plan book as much as I do and look forward to seeing what's coming up next.

After my class has settled in for a few days, I ask the children to find their birthdays in my plan book. I place a special sticker and their name on that date. Having the whole class make a giant greeting card for the birthday child is an ongoing whole language center activity that is used several times a month.

Instructions for the Substitute

Inside the front cover, I tape a statement of my philosophy of teaching, a schedule of special classes, a duty roster, a current class list, and any comments on the special needs of certain children, as well as the names of a few students who can be relied on to help throughout the day. I also tape a picture of myself somewhere inside the cover. It is nice to be able to place a face with the name of the teacher the sub is filling in for. When I have a substitute, I feel confident that I have all the contingencies covered and that my students will experience maximum consistency in their school day while I am away.

I also keep an updated folder of activities labeled "SUBSTITUTE" in the back of my plan book in case the sub needs extra ideas to keep my students engaged during the day. These consist of complete sets of math extensions, creative writing activities, science experiments, getting-to-know-you games, and simple art activities. I keep a copy of a little paperback, *Survival Kit for Substitutes*, by Vita Pavlich and Eleanor Rosenast, for the substitute to browse through at lunch. It is loaded with quick activities to keep children engaged, and it gets borrowed a lot.

Keeping Track of Great Ideas

I frequently find wonderful new projects in professional journals and books that I want to try later in the year. If the article is in one of my own magazines, I cut it out. If it is in a book, I jot it down on a 3-x-5 index card. I staple or paper-clip these gems on the appropriately dated page of my plan book. Some teachers keep a set of dated folders for this purpose. An index card file box works well too. I find that if I don't cut up my teaching magazines into the pieces I want to try, they just pile up somewhere and never get the use they deserve.

Staying Flexible

Write your lesson plans in pencil. Rarely will you get through a week without several changes, for one reason or another. Teachers who would rather fight than switch may be very inflexible, trying to move students too quickly or too slowly through the curriculum. Be open and ready to capitalize on the unexpected. Teachable moments happen every day. Practice becoming more aware of the bird in the window. When events occur that capture your class's attention, use that interest to present new information. Real-life experiences are the richest opportunities for teaching and learning.

One beautiful October afternoon, my class of 27 second-graders went for a neighborhood leaf walk. Their task was to collect colorful leaves for an art and science project. Walking back to school through an alley, Adam spotted a curious object lying near a garbage dumpster. It was the whitened, lower jawbone of some animal, teeth still intact. I could have responded with horror and disgust as Adam picked it up and showed it to his classmates, who were totally enthralled by his find. I did not. They brought it back to school.

After everyone had examined it thoroughly, I placed it on the overhead projector, which created an oversized, silhouetted image on which the entire class could focus, and they spent the rest of the day writing *The Mystery of the Jawbone* (fig. 2.1, p. 28). Each child contributed a theory as to what animal it had belonged to, how that animal lived and died, and how the jawbone happened to end up near our school. Completed with wonderful artwork, they had their first class book of the year. That publication was borrowed for home reading by every child in the class many times. Those children are now in junior high school and still come to visit and ask to see *The Mystery of the Jawbone*.

They did complete their leaf project–three days later. The jawbone and the resulting book appeared nowhere in my lesson plan book.

Fig. 2.1. *The Mystery of the Jawbone.*

Starting a Memory Album

Start taking snapshots of your students as soon as school starts. Ask your principal if there is a petty cash fund for such expenditures. Have someone take a few pictures of you in the classroom, too. A class photograph album creates a sense of family, and students will come back to see you every year to reminisce as you flip through the pages of their memories and yours. Reprints of particularly poignant pictures make a wonderful and personal addition to the final report cards of the year. Create a bulletin board of current photos and add a few to the message board.

Photo-Documenting Special Events

I sometimes photograph my students in costumes that typify a particular unit of study to place on the cover of a folder or book they are compiling. Just recently my third-graders studied Ancient Egypt. When their study was completed, they each donned a felt Egyptian costume and mask, purchased very cheaply after Halloween last fall at a toy store. I took each child's photograph, had them enlarged, and presented them at our Egyptian feast, the culminating activity for our unit.

Another fun project is to design, on a posterboard, bodies of characters you are studying—but cut child-size holes where the heads would be. The children stick their heads in the holes and pose for their unit picture. This was especially amusing after our study of frogs and toads. Our American Indian unit inspired us to create a posterboard with a chief and princess.

Keepsakes like these are reminders of information learned years down the road. I tell my children to keep this kind of memorabilia in their underwear drawer for safekeeping. Nobody ever cleans out the underwear drawer! For 275 other photography ideas, send for *Teaching Tips from Kodak*, Kodak, Consumer Markets Division, Rochester, NY 14650.

Learning Students' Names Quickly

Learning your students' names quickly is imperative to immediate classroom management, building self-esteem, and establishing cohesiveness. There are many ways to speed up the process. Putting names with faces the first day may be easier if you use the following method. Obtain your class list as soon as possible. Take it home and practice saying the first and last names aloud a few times each evening. Write every name in at least three different ways before the first day (e.g., cursive, print, calligraphy, oversized, undersized, in crayon, marker, ink, chalk, pencil, etc.). Close your eyes and visualize each name after it is written. The one drawback to this method is that on the first day of class you may have one or more children tell you that they don't want to be called by their given names and would prefer that you call them by their nicknames. Then it's back to the drawing board to practice again. Believe it or not, there are some children, especially in kindergarten and first grade, who do not even recognize the names under which they were enrolled by their parents. In this time of frequent divorce and remarriage, enrollment names can be quite confusing to children. If you have mastered at least 75 percent of your class list by the end of the first day, you are doing really well. As you take the roll for the first few days, pencil in a few notes to yourself about the appearance of each child. At the end of each day, review each name and do a visual recall of each face. By the end of the second or third day you will know everyone quite well. One teacher I know uses the first names of her third-graders as her first spelling list for the year—very helpful for both her and her students. Always keep a copy of your class list with addresses and telephone numbers, at home. You may want or need to make evening contact with your students or their parents.

Looking at Students' Office Files

Some teachers look through all of their students' office folders before they meet the children for the first time. If this is your choice, keep in mind that every teacher perceives and relates to children differently. For better or worse, you may be fairly warned about Jesse or Molly by their previous teachers. There is always a lot of lounge talk before the school year begins and, for whatever reasons, some veteran teachers will give you, the new kid on the block, a little needling about some of the students you will have. It would be wise to ask your principal if any of the students in your class have special needs. Try not to let the previous teachers' comments shadow your preconceptions of your children. A child who was a behavior problem last year may be a model student for you. Likewise, a student who has never had problems in the past may suddenly begin to act out in your class.

I prefer to look at the records only after I have been with my class for at least one week. Unless there is an obvious medical or emotional problem, I like to look at my students through my own eyes and with my own instincts. I caution you now, and throughout your career, to carefully avoid the temptation to discuss your students and their family problems openly in the teachers' lounge or elsewhere. It is very unprofessional and reflects poorly on your personal integrity. Sometimes teachers get into the Can-You-Top-This game. Limit your questions and comments to staff members who are relevant to each child and hold these conversations privately.

First Contact with Parents and Students

Most schools have a stockpile of stationery and envelopes preprinted with the school's name, address, phone number, and perhaps even a picture of the school mascot. Most principals will be pleased to supply these materials, as well as postage stamps, for the purpose of contacting parents and children prior to the first day of school. Communicating with parents and children the week before school starts is well worth the extra time and effort it takes. It increases everyone's comfort level and breaks the ice for you and your future students.

You can do this with evening telephone calls, too. A phone call might sound something like this:

Hello. This is Miss Smith calling from Lincoln Elementary School. I will have Johnny in my second-grade class this year and I wanted you to know how much I am looking forward to working with you and your son. If you would like to come to school on August 29 to meet with me, I will be available from 8:30 to 11:00 that day to answer any of your questions. Or you can call me any school day at 555-2099 during my planning period from 10:00 to 10:30. I hope to meet you soon. Please tell Johnny that I called and that I will see him on September 1 at 8:30.

I usually start the year with a personal letter to each family.

August 23

Dear Family of _____,

School will be starting again on Tuesday, September 3, and I want you to know how much I am looking forward to working with your child and your family. I have planned a year filled with exciting activities for our class and invite you to visit our room whenever you can. I am available to talk with you from 9:30–10:00 a.m. each school day at 555-0076. I welcome your questions, comments, concerns and suggestions.

Our class will meet from 8:00 a.m. to 2:45 p.m. each day. Music and Physical Education classes will be 9:30–10:00 daily. Lunch is from 11:30–12:05 and morning recess is 10:00–10:15. Your child will bring home more information as soon as school begins.

I will be with your child for approximately 1,000 hours over the coming school year. I would like to meet all of you personally during the next few weeks so that we can plan for your child's individual needs. We have a common interest: the growth and development of your child.

If possible, please allow your child to choose a family photograph to bring to school on the first day. We will be making a class bulletin board using these pictures, for our first art and social studies unit. Our theme will be "HOME IS WHERE ONE STARTS FROM."

Sincerely,

(Signature)

Making Your Correspondence Unique

There is a delightful selection of rubber stamps on the market in greeting card and gift shops. Find one that particularly reflects your distinct personality and use it to sign off on this letter and all of your correspondence to parents throughout the year (fig. 2.2). Stamping your notes, letters, and even report cards adds a personal touch and a spot of color. Someday, you may want to have a rubber stamp made of your signature. During the years ahead, you will write your name thousands of times. With a stamp, you can make quick work of report cards, notes, books, and personalizing other materials. If you accompany your signature with a distinctive stamp, parents will be able to separate your notes from the multitude of other school messages that are sent home daily with their children. Prepare ahead for quick notes by stamping each page of a small note pad. Always date everything you send home.

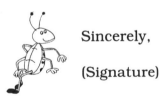

Fig. 2.2. Example of a stamp.

Including Your Photo in Parent Letter

If you have a small, wallet-size photo of yourself to enclose with each letter, so much the better. Photo services advertise in the back of grocery store magazines and make multiple copies of your original for a very reasonable price. The service I currently use is Express Photo, Reliance Color Labs, Inc. Studio j40-7, Box 1000, Swansea, MA 02777 (40 wallet size for $3.50 + $1.00 handling)—cheap and fast! They have been around for years and the quality is surprisingly good.

Almost all schools employ a professional photographer to come in once a year and take individual pictures of students and staff members. If you don't have a suitable photo now, you undoubtedly will by next year. Children love to have their own personal wallet picture of their teacher. I always throw a few in my Treasure Box and am surprised how quickly they are taken.

Getting Your Correspondence Pre-Approved

Many schools request that most letters, such as the one on page 31, and most other written communications to parents, be given to the principal for proofreading and approval. If you have no such rule, have a fellow teacher look over your correspondence to check for spelling or grammatical errors. Nothing is quite as embarrassing or unprofessional as letters from a teacher that contain these kinds of mistakes. Far better to have your errors caught in-house than to be apprised of them by one of your student's parents. Keep a small dictionary in your desk at all times and by all means check your written documents carefully before sending them out.

First Meetings with Parents

Every year several parents respond to the invitation to come in and discuss their child's needs. Even though statistically only 3 percent of the general population falls in the gifted and talented category of intelligence, I am informed by at least 25 percent of my parents that their child is performing in this range. I listen patiently and congratulate them sincerely on their good fortune; then, with a few key questions, I try to determine the child's specific talents or interests and, more importantly, the parent's expectations for me and their child. Subsequently, I plan lessons and activities throughout the year to encourage enrichment of these interests and to include parental involvement. I tell these parents I am most happy to provide an individualized, quality, and challenging education for their youngster within the time constraints of my obligations to all students. It is not up to me to judge who is talented and who isn't. Parents *do* know their children best, and I would rather work with parents who hold their children in highest regard than those who are not the least interested in what happens to their children once they enter school.

Other parents want me to be aware of special physical needs, ranging from peanut butter allergies to seizure disorders. And, joy of joys, I almost always have a talented homemaker who loves to volunteer time and help with class parties and field trips. Grab this person fast!

Conclusion

The time you spend on the ideas in this chapter before the hectic part of the school year begins, will benefit you throughout the year. Overpreparation is the key to your success and peace of mind in the coming weeks. There simply won't be time to backtrack to some of these projects once the children have arrived to fill your every working moment with their needs and demands.

Resources

(Note: The asterisk [*] denotes titles I believe are most helpful to first year teachers.)

*Eisele, Beverly. *Managing the Whole Language Classroom: A Complete Teaching Resource Guide for K-6 Teachers.* Cypress, Calif.: Creative Teaching Press, 1991.

Evertson, Carolyn M., Edmund T. Emmer, Barbara S. Clements, Julie P. Sanford, and Murray E. Worsham. *Classroom Management for Elementary Teachers.* Needham Heights, Mass.: Allyn & Bacon, 1989.

*Harrison, Ann Salisbury, and Frances Burton Spuler. *Hot Tips for Teachers.* New York: Simon & Schuster, 1983.

Jones, Vernon F., and Louise S. Jones. *Comprehensive Classroom Management.* Needham Heights, Mass.: Allyn & Bacon, 1990.

Larson, Knute, and James McGoldrick. *Handbook of School Letters.* West Nyack, N.Y.: Parker, 1970.

Pavlich, Vita, and Eleanor Rosenast. *Survival Kit for Substitutes.* New York: Scholastic Magazines, 1974.

3
Go! The First Day

Read this chapter *slowly*, more than once. Close your eyes and visualize each activity, as if you were actually in your own classroom with your own students. If you are feeling overwhelmed by the multitude of ideas being presented, take a break and set this chapter aside for awhile. Remember, too, that many of these ideas and activities will be part of your classroom routine throughout the year, and will become just that—routine. My goal is to forewarn you of pitfalls encountered by many new teachers and therefore offer a schedule that can forestall problems before they occur.

The Night Before

Set your alarm clock an hour early the night before the first day—you will probably not sleep well anyway! The day you have waited and prepared for is almost here. You will want to spend a little extra time on your grooming in the morning. Knowing you look your best will boost your confidence and give you one less thing

to worry about. After 31 first days, I still find I am restless and excited the night before a new school year begins. Every year presents new faces, new personalities, and new challenges. In spite of many days of preparation, you will think of at least five more things you wish you had done. Get to school very early and get a few of the more urgent last-minute items completed.

I offer one way you may approach your first day in the classroom. My agenda is highly personalized, as yours will be. Use the elements that suit your style, add your own, and delete the others. Be well prepared and overly organized the first few days, and always plan too many rather than too few activities. The best technique for classroom management is to keep children too engaged to even think of inappropriate behaviors. Read the chapter on centers (chapter 6). Set up two or three centers of general interest before the first day.

Know Where You're Headed

One of your fundamental goals is to firmly impart your clearly defined expectations: the first minute, the first hour, the entire day. Don't assume that your students will come to you knowing how to behave in a school setting. It has been well documented that the teachers who are the most effective classroom managers begin each day promptly in a businesslike manner, use a set routine, perform daily chores such as roll call efficiently, present lessons clearly, and demonstrate respect for learning and the learners. Children will perceive you as friendly, predictable, reliable, and someone who values their feelings.

Consider asking yourself these questions when deciding what your expectations will be:

1. What kind of emotional climate do I want to create for my classroom?

2. What kind of physical appearance do I want to present to children?

3. What will the physical climate of my classroom be?

4. What values do I want to foster in my students?

5. How much of myself am I willing to share with children and their families?

6. Will I be consistent about the parameters I have set?

7. Will my students leave here each day feeling good about themselves?

8. Will they be eager to return to me tomorrow?

Because there are so many details to cover when school begins, I find it best to dispense all of this new information in small doses. Never again will you be doing as much talking *to* children as you will on this day, although many of these tasks and activities will be repeated every day. Plan to have several short meetings with your students throughout the day and to use several minutes modeling and rehearsing daily routine procedures such as lining up, raising hands, getting drinks, and so on. These meetings may be conducted while children are in their seats, but my own personal style is to call them to the rug each time. Following is a suggested format for the first day's activities.

A Schedule for the First Day

The first day will consist of several lengthy, informational meetings but they are necessary so that you can firmly establish your image as an assured and well-ordered adult, a teacher on whom your students can rely. A turbulent, wishy-washy first day will result in many headaches by the end of the first week and thereafter. Your first day may go something like this:

GETTING STARTED

1. Seating the children
2. Talking to the parents
3. New students
4. Private meetings
5. My rules—Your rules—Our rules
6. Behavior management
7. Restroom procedures
8. Recess procedures
9. Touring the classroom
10. First whole-class activity
11. First recess
12. Culminating the first whole-class activity

BEFORE-LUNCH ACTIVITIES

1. Touring the building
2. Classroom library
3. First story
4. Name games
5. Pledge of allegiance

LUNCH PROCEDURES

AFTER-LUNCH ACTIVITIES

1. Post discussion of lunch
2. Daily schedule
3. Sharing
4. First assignment
5. Turning in work
6. Music and gym procedures

END-OF-DAY ACTIVITIES

1. Review the day
2. Finish story
3. Papers to go home
4. Bait for tomorrow and farewell

Getting Started

Seating the Children

The arrival and dismissal of children on the first day is handled in as many different ways as there are schools, and your principal will discuss the procedures with you. When you finally take the children into your classroom, the countdown is at lift-off and you are on your own at last. Assuming that you have an individual desk for each child, you can make seating assignments in several ways:

1. Upon entering the room, each child finds a desk of his or her own choosing, for the time being.

2. Children find their seats by looking for name tags placed on each desk by you.

3. Children are assigned desks by alphabetical order.

4. Children gather first at the meeting area of your room for introductions and roll call.

The seating arrangements will be temporary for the first part of the day, but more permanent assignments should be made by the second day, or at least by the end of the first week. You will want to observe closely how children are responding to each other and make changes accordingly as you learn how each child functions in the classroom. You will be surprised how quickly the students establish their territory and begin building friendships. Allowing good friends to sit near each other—and they *will* ask—has its merits and drawbacks, so ultimately you will have to judge the feasibility of each individual situation. You will undoubtedly regroup many times as the year progresses to facilitate cooperative learning groups, compatibility, and buddy systems. There is nothing sacred about keeping desks in straight rows. Consider trying desks in one large circle; small circles; pods of two, three, four, or six; a horseshoe shape; or a semicircle.

Be watchful for children who are squinting at boardwork or things you are presenting from a distance. Some children will need preferential seating because of vision, hearing, or behavior problems. Special education students who are mainstreamed or integrated into your class may need several modifications in curriculum as well as seating. The teaching specialists will help you with all of your questions concerning these children. Don't ever hesitate to ask for any help you need; even veteran teachers need ongoing assistance with these students. Each child presents new and unique challenges to us all.

Talking to the Parents

So . . . now everyone is seated and you have a few parents eagerly awaiting what you have to say. If you have already contacted your students' families by phone or letter, your self-introduction will be brief. If you haven't, you can introduce yourself and write your name on the board. In any case, you will want to offer your welcome to everyone in the room and express your pleasure in finally meeting everyone. You might offer a very brief statement of your philosophy and expectations for the year. A good icebreaker is to take attendance and have each child who is accompanied by parents introduce the visitors to you and the class.

Make a note to yourself in your attendance book about the parents who are here on this first day and perhaps a brief comment on their physical appearance so you will be able to call them by name the next time you meet (e.g., "Mom, tall blonde," or "Dad, bearded, short"). I often have had difficulty matching parents with children the first few weeks if I have a large class. It is helpful for positive public relations and personal comfort to be able to call people by name when you meet unexpectedly on the playground or in the grocery store. Whatever method you use, make sure you learn parents' names as quickly as possible.

Before parents leave, discuss the daily schedule, which you have already written on the board, and the supply list. Tell them their child will be bringing home copies of this information and much more at the end of the day. You may also inform them of times you are available for conferencing and give a phone number where you can be reached. I have always given my home phone number to parents in case of emergencies and have never had my privacy intruded upon by students or their families. This, of course, is a matter of personal choice and circumstances for you.

◆ The Parent Who Doesn't Leave

In the primary grades, particularly in kindergarten, you may have a child and a parent who have a difficult time separating from each other on the first day of school. Teachers handle this situation in many different ways, and you of course must do what is most comfortable for you. Some teachers invite parents to remain in the classroom on the first day for a set amount of time while they explain school procedures, supply needs, and whatever else they want to discuss. Then they ask that the parents leave and return for their children at the end of the session or school day. For most parents, this works quite well. Other teachers have no set rules for parent visitation, and may have them remain for a while and quietly leave when they feel that all is well for their child.

For several years, I taught preschool physically handicapped children who began coming to our class on their third birthdays. It was quite understandable that parents were reluctant to leave their special little ones on the first day, or even during the first week. I encouraged these parents to stay as long as they needed to and asked them to be helpers. After a couple of days, there was usually a mutual decision for them to spend less time in the classroom during each session. As their confidence in me as an educator and alternate care provider for their handicapped child increased, their need to be present diminished. Parents never stayed in the classroom for more than a few days. With parents and their children who are feeling insecure about a new situation, you are responsible for establishing a bond of trust and comfort. Constantly put yourself in the other person's place, treat them as you would want to be treated, and you'll rarely go wrong. The majority of children you will be teaching have probably been in a school or day-care setting prior to attending your class, but for the child who knows nothing but home and Mom or Dad, the first day of school can be frightening and even traumatic, if not handled gently and professionally by you.

Go ahead with your plans for the day; make it look like you're all having a great time (for you will be), and let the rest of your students' demeanors be contagious for your reluctant children. Keep the invitation for them to join you and the rest of the class quite open, obvious, and enticing. Let them make the next move. Remember, you can always consult with your principal, school social worker, or psychologist in the rare event that a child or family has behaviors far beyond rational limits.

Let all parents know they are welcome to visit your class any time. It can be very upsetting for parents to be told they must make an appointment to visit your class. You will soon become accustomed to people dropping in unannounced, although, in all likelihood, this won't happen often.

At this point, you may ask for any further questions and tell parents to feel free to leave or stay, whichever is most comfortable and convenient for them, and that you are now proceeding with the day's activities with the children. Very rarely will a parent stay beyond this subtle signal that you are in control of the situation.

New Students

Many students will be new to your school, and this year you will share a special bond with them because your inner experiences will be so similar. Try never to forget this feeling of insecurity mixed with excitement. By next year, you will feel like an old pro, but you will again have students who have never been to your school before. They will need your empathy and understanding. Hopefully, you will never forget what it felt like to be the new kid on the block. Use all your energy and flair on this day. Your first day of teaching should be like an opening night on Broadway. The tone you set now will follow you for the rest of the year. Your first school year is well under way!

Private Meetings

During your first meeting with your children, tell them that you know there may be times when they need to speak with you privately and that you will always make yourself available as soon as possible. Give them a few examples of topics they need to discuss with you only, such as family problems.

Become very familiar with your school's policies on reporting suspected child abuse or neglect. There are very specific and binding procedures for such reports; usually the school's policy handbook will spell these out in detail. Your responsibilities in this area are very serious and have legal ramifications that could affect your future career in teaching. Ask for all the information you need to make responsible decisions.

I ask my students to state simply, "I need to talk to you!" I immediately give them a specific time and place to meet alone with me. This is usually during recess or before or after school, which ensures privacy, doesn't interfere with my attention to the rest of the class, and cuts back the requests from children who just like to chat. Students usually will not miss recess for anything short of a serious problem. Be prepared to listen to and handle some very interesting stories.

My Rules—Your Rules—Our Rules

My rules are few, explicit, and non-negotiable:

1. Everyone in our room is always treated with respect.

2. We need to know when you leave the room.

3. We will listen courteously when anyone speaks.

4. We always walk in the school. (Yes, Johnny, the playground and gym are exceptions!)

You undoubtedly noticed that the words *no* and *never* are missing. Try to phrase your rules in a positive manner. Implied by these few simple rules are NO HITTING (1.), GET PERMISSION TO LEAVE THE ROOM (2.), NO TALKING OUT OF TURN (3.), NO RUNNING (4.). Many infractions are covered under rule 1, and my students and I will discuss them at length. If a child abuses a rule, I restate it, the child repeats it for me, and we talk about how he or she can keep from breaking that rule in the future. The children soon understand that rules make spending time together safe and comfortable for all of us. Make it clear that there are *no* exceptions.

Behavior Management

Consistency is the secret to making these rules the only ones needed to maintain acceptable behavior. Never be too busy to stop immediately and review a rule when it is broken. Consider using Time Out, discussed below, for children who are not able to abide by rules with this casual approach. Other widely used discipline plans are also reviewed later in this chapter for your consideration. Be sure to check with your principal before using any such program. Your school probably has its own unique system for monitoring student behavior, but I offer these as examples of programs that have worked well for others. There are also several other sources of information on this subject in the Resources section at the end of this chapter.

◆ Keeping Parents Informed

Send a letter to parents soon after school begins, informing them of your classroom rules and explaining any behavior management techniques you will be using. This will avoid misunderstandings later on in the year. If you decide to use Time Out, you might even send copies of this method to the parents so they will understand exactly how it works. They may even choose to use it at home; parents will frequently seek your advice about a discipline routine for their child. Again, refer to this chapter's Resources section for books parents might like to read on this subject.

Over the next few days, we have many class meetings when the children can propose rules they feel they need. Later, by the end of the second week, we reach consensus and post a chart listing the parameters by which we can all be happiest. Keep your list of rules as short and concise as possible. Small children can rarely remember more than five or six at a time.

◆ Time Out

Almost every teacher and parent has used Time Out in some form or another for years. You may even remember standing in the corner or going to your room when you were a child. In schools, children are sometimes sent to stand in the hall or to the principal's office. Although these steps may make the teacher feel a little better for the moment, they really do nothing to change the child's understanding of the situation.

Children must learn to become more aware of their inappropriate behaviors and the consequences those behaviors incur. They need to be dealt with in a humane way by the adults in their lives.

Time Out Procedure:

1. PLACE A CHAIR where it can be seen by you but not by the child's peers, in a seldom-used section of the room, perhaps beside your filing cabinet or desk. Never put children in the hall or anywhere else where you cannot monitor them.

2. EXPLAIN the Time Out procedure to the entire class well before you ever need to use it, so that it is not instituted at a time when it will be directed at one particular student or when you are feeling too angry or frustrated. Tell the students that you will be using it whenever someone in the class is in need of learning more appropriate behaviors and taking time to make better decisions about themselves.

3. When told to go to the Time Out chair, the child is to go immediately, without discussion. The best procedure is to have a timer set for one minute for each year of the child's age (e.g., an eight-year-old would take eight minutes out). After the timer rings, the teacher goes to the child to confer.

4. DISCUSS these questions with the child:

   a. Why were you sent to Time Out? (Discuss the broken rule and have the child repeat it to you.)

   b. What is your side of the story? (This lets the child know that you are willing to listen.)

   c. What do you think would be appropriate consequences for this behavior? (This helps children to accept responsibility and empowers them to choose their own fate. Usually Time Out is all that is needed.)

This technique has been used very effectively in classrooms in which children with emotional problems have been mainstreamed, as well as with "normal" children. In most cases, students will need to use Time Out on only one or two occasions, if the classroom climate is so stimulating and comfortable that the child values the missing class time.

The teacher is never put in the position of having to reprimand a student in front of peers. It saves students' dignity and teachers' energy. A simple "Please take Time Out" is all that need be said. Eventually, some students will even prevent negative situations by telling you they need Time Out in order to maintain appropriate behavior. Some teachers occasionally signal the entire class to a Time

Out period when some incident has disrupted the group. This is done by turning out the classroom lights and setting the timer for a few minutes. Have students put their heads down on the desks for a few quiet moments to bring the class back to readiness.

◆ The Marble Jar

You can make a contract with your class to reinforce positive behaviors by keeping a marble jar in a conspicuous place in the room. As you notice appropriate behaviors, place a marble in the jar. When the jar is filled, the entire class is rewarded with an extra recess, a free time, game time, or some other meaningful celebration. Small children should only be required to fill a small jar.

◆ Behavior Desk Charts

Individual behavior can be monitored by taping a chart or segmented picture, such as a train with many cars, a flower with many petals, or the like, to each child's desk. Throughout the day, as you circulate around the room, you (and only you) can fill in a segment of each child's chart as you observe such things as neat handwriting, quiet reading, an orderly activity, one child helping another, or whatever else you are trying to reinforce. A completed chart or picture usually requires about one week's effort, and in my class warrants a trip to the Treasure Box. This is a very effective, personal, and quiet method of monitoring behaviors.

◆ The Checkmark System

With any behavior modification program, it is critical that you be consistent and clear with all procedures and consequences. Also be sure that your techniques are compatible with your school's policies and those of any teammates. In most schools, when inappropriate behavior is a persistent problem, inconsistency and ambiguity are usually present as well. My motto is, "Say what you mean and mean what you say!" Once you have firmly established your classroom rules, you may want to consider this alternative method for maintaining discipline.

1st time a rule is broken = name on a sheet of paper on the teacher's desk

2nd time rule is broken = 1 checkmark by name = 10 minutes after school

3rd time rule is broken = 2 checkmarks by name = 15 minutes after school

4th time rule is broken = 3 checkmarks by name and parent is contacted

5th time rule is broken = 4 checkmarks, parent contact, and meeting with the principal

If you are reaching the three checkmark stage repeatedly with a primary-age child, confer with the parents frequently and try to develop a plan to get to the root of the child's problems, perhaps with the help of the school social worker. Rarely should you have to go beyond steps 1 and 2 with a young child.

◆ Other Behavior Management Techniques

Keeping children after school is not allowed in some schools, or busing may make this arrangement impossible. Your school may also have a designated area where supervision is provided for children who need to have time away from the classroom. If so, you might shorten lunch recess instead of keeping the child after school.

Many children who are acting out in class will respond most positively to a little extra attention from you, by which you acknowledge that you have noticed they are having a difficult time with school rules. Over and over again I have had the most success with these students by having a conference with them as soon as negative behaviors show a definite pattern. This is usually evident in the first or second week. I have several special job routines in my room that offer children added self-esteem. Every year, after a private conference, I give the coveted job of audiovisual coordinator to my most difficult student. He or she becomes the sole person in charge of getting and returning films to the office, plugging in any media tool we are using that day, stringing films onto the projector and rewinding them when we are finished, and helping me with many other responsible chores having to do with audiovisual equipment. The classroom behavior improves immediately. If the behavior slips a little, a few gentle reminders that I am counting on that student to help me throughout the year are usually all that are needed. Taking special care of pets, walking the class rabbit on his leash at recess, erasing boards, taking attendance, being the fire drill captain or a messenger to the office, and helping with a handicapped classmate are some of the jobs in my classroom given to children who need an extra boost in self-concept. I do not use these special tasks to reward inappropriate behavior. They must be earned by showing a positive behavior change.

But there *was* the little boy for whom nothing else worked. He was an incorrigible spitter and was abhorred by his classmates. He responded to none of my tried-and-true methods. Finally, in desperation, I set before him a Mason jar and asked that he fill it so that I could show his parents what a prolific *and* wonderful spitter he was. That was the end of the spitting. I also had a child who delighted in shocking us with inappropriate body noises. Again, after all else failed, I asked him to stay after school for a few minutes to tape-record all the wonderful noises he made at school so we could replay them for his family. That, too, was the end of that! I hope you'll never be this desperate. Sometimes you just have to be downright creative. (No, the jar was never filled and the tape recording was never made.)

Restroom Procedures

If you are following the suggested agenda for your first class meeting, at this point you will begin to see the telltale signs of a pressing need to take care of restroom procedures in the near future.

Ask the children to walk to the classroom door and form two lines, boys and girls. This may take a few rehearsals. In your best hushed voice, explain the necessity to walk quietly through the hall, use the restrooms quickly, flush (yes, you will need to tell them), wash hands, return to the line, and follow you back to the classroom in the same quiet manner.

No, everyone need not use the restroom at the same time, particularly in kindergarten and first grade. Your school may have specific procedures, but they may not appear in your handbook, so ask another primary teacher about them.

◆ A Pass System

You may find that your school has a pass system. Each teacher may have a set of hallway passes of some sort so that a limited number of children are authorized to be in the restrooms, the office, or on errands at any one time. Unless a child has a physical or medical problem, he or she usually will be able to take care of any needs before school starts, during recess, at lunch time, and perhaps with pass permission once or twice a day. If a child asks more frequently than this, you need to investigate the cause, as he or she is missing too much class time.

◆ The Missing Child

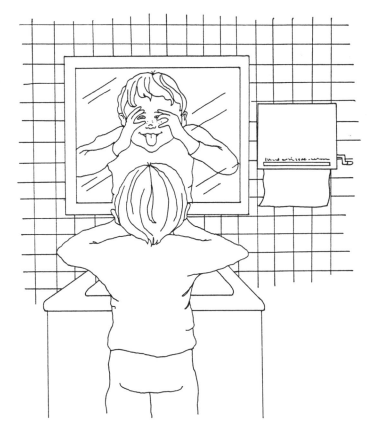

A child who is missing after a restroom trip could be ill—but more probably is a "Looky Loo," wanting to see what's happening around the school. This child may be making faces in the mirrors and performing other noneducational activities, such as echo-testing in the restroom stalls. He or she may also be strolling up and down the hall, checking backpacks and coat pockets, or peeking into or lingering at the doors of other classes. Three minutes is my standard time limit for pass trips to the restroom. No complaints have ever been registered. That's just how it is, folks, in our room!

Getting Drinks

Unless a child is choking, gasping, or has a persistent cough, I put limits on trips to the drinking fountain. I once had a girl who was going to the drinking fountain in the hall every ten minutes and not returning for five more. When I curtailed her frequent absences, her mother complained bitterly that the child needed to drink a lot of water for medical reasons. I could not convince her that her daughter was also dilly-dallying to avoid working in the classroom. I solved the problem by providing a thermos of water and a drinking cup at the child's desk. Her consumption of H_2O dropped dramatically after the first day of this new method. After you know your children for a few days, you'll set your own workable parameters.

Recess Procedures

Well before your first recess, explain the procedures you will be following. Recess is sacred children's time and you may look forward to this breather as much as the kids do. Many teachers use this time for one-on-one teaching and may keep one or two students with them. This is appropriate if it is the child's choice to stay in and work. In all honesty, I doubt that very many primary children would choose this option.

◆ Keeping Children in from Recess

If a child has wasted the time to complete an assignment or has been a behavior problem, punishing the child by having him or her miss recess is a poor choice of disciplinary action. Too often, you will pass a classroom where children are kept in for recess as a form of punishment, and you will soon notice that the same children are in the same room day after day *after day*. Obviously, this type of classroom management does not work, or children would stay in only once or twice at the most. Later in the year, if you have a couple of children who are unable to finish assigned seatwork, even though they seem to be on task most of the time, you may need to reassess the amount of work you are giving these children. Students who go out to speech, special education, music lessons, Chapter I classes, or other pull-out programs should always be given abbreviated assignments. How unfair it would be to expect them to complete the same amount of classroom work as children who never leave the room! These children are put into special classes because it has been determined that they need extra instruction, not extra seatwork. Ten addition and subtraction problems completed accurately is proof enough that they have the right idea, doing thirty more problems does little for them or for me. They need a recess as much and usually more than the other children in the class.

Recess is the time for children to get sorely needed gross motor activity, to talk as loudly as they wish, and just be *kids*! Denying children recess time may only multiply the problems for them and you, as well.

Explain that upon your announcement, "It is recess time," children should retrieve jackets, sweaters, and playground equipment and line up (or follow whatever procedure you use in your building). If you haven't already had an all-school assembly informing children of the playground rules, now is the time to do so. These will be in print somewhere; if not, ask to be on a committee to help formulate and standardize a policy for your school. Be specific about the playground rules and the consequences of not following them.

Many serious injuries occur on the playground, but most can be avoided by adhering to safety regulations. Again, seek clarification before your first recess is upon you.

Remind children to use the restrooms if necessary. Give positive reinforcement for remembering to use the restrooms at the appropriate time when they return to the classroom after recess.

Touring the Classroom

By this time of your first day, your students are more than ready to get up and move around their new classroom. Take them on a tour of the room, opening cabinets, closets, and drawers, explaining what is where and why. Briefly tell them how each space can be used and encourage questions and comments. As you explain each area, role-play a student thinking out loud; "I need some red paper, so I go to this cabinet, get what I need, and get back to my project. I broke my pencil. I can get a sharpened one from this drawer without asking my teacher or interrupting my neighbors. I'll just leave this old one in this box and get back to my assignments."

First Whole-Class Activity

Your first class activity should be one in which all students will experience individual success, heightened self-esteem, and a sense of fun, as well as contribute to a sense of community. Of course, all activities throughout the year should have the same goals. A very successful first project is the making of name tags for desks, the teacher's included.

Gather the children back on the rug, set up your overhead projector, and model several ways in which to create a name tag that is unique and personal. Show how to make an attractive border, or several borders if you have the time. Have a good time demonstrating and let your enthusiasm be contagious in this and all projects. Color and decorate your name and save a little space at the end of the tag to make your own special symbol (a flower, a book, a kite, a ball, etc.). Ask the children to think of a symbol that would be special to put next to their names. Pass out a 4-x-12 oaktag strip to each child and put coloring materials in a central location to be shared by students who have not yet brought their own school supplies. For very young children, you might want to pencil in their names for them beforehand. First names are usually sufficient for this project.

Send the students to their seats and start being a real kid watcher. You may want to have the children bring their tags back to the rug and do a show-and-tell, or you may immediately tape the tags to the corners of the desks as they are completed. Children should feel free to wander from desk to desk to see what their classmates have created. If you have access to a laminating machine, cover the name tags as soon as possible so they will last all year.

During recess, look at all the name tags made by the children. Using a class list, note all the symbols chosen. You will use this information after morning recess.

First Recess

About this time, you will probably have your first recess period. You will have discussed procedures before the name tag art activity, so everyone knows what to expect. If possible, go out to recess with your students this first time so that you can observe and help with supervision. Your staff will probably share playground duties on a rotating schedule, which will be given to you the week before school begins. For today, though, stay as close to your class as possible. During the next 10 to 15 minutes you will learn a great deal about how your children relate to each other.

Culminating the First Whole-Class Activity

After recess, ask children to return to their desks to discuss the name tag activity. Call on the children, one by one—who drew a flower, for example, as a symbol. Ask them to say their full name, why they chose their particular symbol, and what is their favorite color on the name tag they designed.

This is a low-risk activity for speaking before the entire class for the first time. The child remains seated at the desk, has a physical focus (the name tag), and there are no wrong answers. Most children will be quite comfortable with this activity.

The Right to Pass

When doing any project that requires children to divulge personal information, you must offer them the option to *pass*. They can simply say, "I pass," knowing there will be no pressure to actively participate. This is an acceptable and desirable refusal skill and should be encouraged. As their teacher and role model, you can and should exercise this option yourself at appropriate times.

The right to pass does not apply to teaching situations in which you are looking for feedback on learning tasks. Demonstrate the difference many times throughout the first few days until the concept is clearly understood. "What is 2 + 4? Spell *cat*. How old are you?" versus "Where did you go last night? How many people live in your house? Did you take a bath last night?"

Before-Lunch Activities

Touring the Building

Line up your class and take them for a sightseeing walk through the building, pointing out important locations along the way. Don't bypass the boiler room and custodian's office. Children are always fascinated with the internal workings of their school. Each year I have asked our custodian to give a tour of the power plant sometime in the spring. It is a fascinating experience and the science, social studies, and art projects that result are always wonderful. The furnace room abounds with geometric shapes and curious noises.

Displaying the Classroom Library

Gather a large selection of reading material from your own resources: the public library, garage sales, yard sales, flea markets, the school library, the district's resource center, friends, neighbors, relatives, Goodwill, and so on. Show children the large variety of books, magazines, comic books, and newspapers you have amassed for their use and briefly explain how and when they may be used. Allow them a few minutes to browse and explore the classroom library. Tomorrow they may begin making selections to keep at their desks or check out to take home.

Provide a container of small slips of paper on which students write the names of the publications they are taking home. Have children deposit these slips in another container. When they return the materials, they remove and discard the slip of paper. If you want a more permanent record of your children's reading habits, keep an index card for each child, punch a hole in the corner, and put all of the cards on a library ring. Write the name of each book read and the date completed on each child's card. These reading records could be put into the childrens' portfolios. Your students will also be checking out books from the school library and will probably have a set time each week for this activity.

Whenever you begin a unit of study, fill a table or bookshelf with all the books and magazines you can find on your topic so that the children have a variety of resource materials to refer to for study, research, and story and report writing. An old coffee table makes an ideal place to display such books, and children just naturally love to be on their knees. Most of the items I am suggesting to supplement your classroom furnishings are usually yours for the asking by sending a wish list home with your students. Parents can usually loan or give you anything you need. You may end up with more than you want, but it doesn't hurt to ask. Someone else on your staff will gladly take any leftovers.

Storytime

Reading to your students for the first time should set the tone for shared reading for the rest of the year. Experts still encourage teachers to read to children for at least 10 minutes every day, regardless of the students' age. It is one of my favorite parts of the day. Remind the students of your expectation that they will listen while you are speaking. It is all right to raise their hands to ask questions or make comments, but they may not interrupt you verbally.

Choose one of your favorite books with a surprise or suspenseful ending. The length of this first story will depend on the attention span of your age group. Read enthusiastically right up to the cliffhanger ending and then *stop*. Ask children to try to predict how they think the story will end. You will finish the story at the end of the day. If you have selected a great book, the children will clamor for you to finish right now, but hold out.

◆ Solving Attention Problems

Children should not be talking with each other during story time. If you have a child who can't listen attentively, you can have him or her sit close to you and be the page turner. Patting the child gently on the shoulder or back in a soothing manner as you read is usually all that is needed to quiet most chatterboxes. Occasionally you will have a child who engages in self-stimulating behavior during periods of passive inactivity. Special-needs children with limited vision are prone to head nodding and rolling during quiet times. Hearing-impaired children need to be close in front of you so they can lip read and cue from the illustrations. These children need to be nearest you so you can use touch signals to reestablish socially appropriate behavior. I once had a very bright second-grade girl with autistic-like behaviors that included frequent sexual autostimulation. It took several private discussions and a behavior modification program before I was able to change this distracting behavior. Check with your special education teachers to see if behavioral programs are already in place for some of your students. You will want to provide consistency for these children.

Name Games

Assuming that you have familiarized yourself with the names of the children on your class list, you now must match faces to those names. Name games will help you and your students get acquainted during the first few days. Here are a few activities that have worked well.

Go around the class until each child has said his or her name and favorite sweet. "My name is Miss Jones and I like chocolate." Other good icebreaking topics are: favorite TV show, color, toy, food, playtime activity, sport, school subject, relative, etc.

This same activity becomes a little more interesting if each person also taps out a rhythm on the desk with a pencil: "My - name is - Tom - my - I like to eat - pop - corn." The entire group then echoes, "His - name is - Tom - my - he likes to eat - pop - corn."

For a ball toss name game, assemble children in a circle. The teacher throws a ball to a student as he says, "My name is Mr. Jones." The child who catches the ball says her name as she tosses the ball to another student. Children could also sit on the floor and roll the ball. You might substitute a beanbag or small pillow for the ball.

Another variation of the name game is to use one describing word about yourself as you say your name. "I'm jolly Miss Jones." "I'm teasing Tommy." Or try saying what animal you would like to be: "I'm Miss Jones, the poodle." You will find many more name games in chapter 4.

Pledge of Allegiance

If you plan to incorporate the pledge of allegiance into your morning opening activity format, now would be a good time to have your first discussion and practice. I have always found the pledge an appropriate way to start the day. It sets the tone for community spirit and respect and is a natural way to bring children down from a before-school playground high. One of the class responsibilities can be the job of flagbearer. A child is chosen to hold the flag each morning for a week. That child brings the class to attention and leads the pledge. At the end of the week, you may issue a little paper American flag for the child to pin to his or her shirt. These flags are available at party or art supply stores and are very inexpensive; they come in packages of tens or twenties.

◆ Some Children Do Not Say the Pledge

Some children do not say the pledge, for religious or other reasons. Hopefully, parents have already informed you of this family preference. Unobtrusively tell these children that you are aware of their choice and ask that they sit or stand quietly until the class is finished. Under no circumstances should they be forced to explain or be ridiculed for their nonparticipation. Remember Class Rule 1: Everyone in our room is treated with respect! If a child challenges, simply explain that in Johnny's family the pledge is not recited, and let it go at that. If you choose to have your class recite the pledge daily, you can begin first thing tomorrow morning.

The Daily Calendar

Most primary classes also start the day by updating the wall calendar. There is a wide variety of calendar grids and colorful cutouts to mark the passage of each day. I often make this daily activity more of a learning experience by laminating a blank calendar grid. The children create the cutouts and then number them. Any birthdays, holidays, vacation days, or other dates of importance are given a special shape or color and are marked with the number of that day. The blank, laminated grid can also be written on with a water-soluble marker in lieu of paper markers.

When You've Lost Their Attention

When I was teaching physically handicapped children, we often put our wheelchair-bound students into a specially designed stand-up table for various activities during the day. This provided a change of position for cramped limbs and backs and a different view of the environment, and always increased intellectual productivity. One of the most unnatural characteristics of modern classroom design is the denial of mobility opportunities to innately mobile little people. Take time frequently to allow your students to move and stretch or even take a little stroll around the room. A few brief seconds of physical activity will result in children who are better able to complete sedentary tasks.

You undoubtedly recall the discomfort and tedium of lengthy college lectures and may soon revive these feelings when you begin attending the many inservices and meetings required of teachers. My personal rule of observation is that if I have lost eye contact with more than three children, or have more than three squirmers, it is time for a change of pace, a little stand-up-and-move-around break, and perhaps a lesson plan change.

Use Body Language

The urge to say, "Sit still! Sit up straight! Pay attention!" is a signal that I have a problem, not my students. Early in the year I establish a nonverbal signaling system that eliminates any need for me to interrupt my interaction with the class. A finger to my lips and eye contact soon stills inappropriate chatting. An exaggerated straightening of my back indicates the need for a posture correction. You will soon develop your own sign language to communicate with your children.

Lunch Procedures

It's been a long and busy morning and some children have undoubtedly been asking when it will be lunch time since approximately 9:10 a.m.! During summer vacation, most children snack whenever they please, and they may not have been up at such an early hour since last June. Many probably were rushed off to school with little or no breakfast. So, let's talk lunch.

Again, check the procedures used in your school and explain them to your class at this time. Most schools provide a hot lunch program, so you will need to take roll and find out who pays for a hot lunch, who orders free or reduced-price lunch, and who has brought lunch from home. In some schools, this money is collected first thing in the morning or is collected on a weekly or monthly basis. You may even have a few students who go home or to a sitter for lunch. Use a separate class list to record this information.

An inexpensive plastic laundry basket makes a sturdy container for lunches. You might also use a cardboard box that your custodian can supply. Let the children decorate this box during some free time in the first few days. Another class responsibility is assigning children to take the lunch basket or box to the lunchroom and return it to class afterward. Explain procedures and modes of conduct expected in the lunchroom and answer any questions. LUNCH AT LAST!

grrr!

Join the children in the lunchroom and eat with them about once a month, or have the children eat with you in the classroom for a real treat! Many teachers use their lunchtime to catch up on paperwork or other chores and eat alone in their classrooms. Unless you are absolutely and hopelessly behind in your work, try to spend this precious time in the teachers' lunchroom, getting acquainted with the staff, sharing experiences, and letting your hair down for a few minutes.

After-Lunch Activities

Reviewing Lunch Procedures

When the children return to the classroom, gather them on the rug once more and talk about the lunch period. Be prepared for complaints. The first lunch period of the year in our school rarely goes as smoothly as everyone would like, but each day will become easier.

Discussing the Daily Schedule

Send the students to their seats and begin going over the daily schedule you have written on the board. For third-graders, you might even supply a duplicated schedule to each child to follow at his or her desk. For younger children, a schedule compiled of rebus pictures works well: a book for reading, a pencil for writing, and so on. Tomorrow morning you will begin to follow this schedule more closely. Remember, though, that schedules are tentative at best. Rarely will a day pass in which you don't have to make one or two changes.

To aid children's understanding, present the schedule in blocks of activity rather than by minutes. Certain activities are usually set in cement, such as music, physical education, library, recesses, and lunch. You can design the rest of the day using your best judgment. If you are team-teaching, you will have less flexibility and must work out a mutually satisfactory schedule. Arranging times for children to attend special classes, such as speech, counseling, special education, Chapter I reading, and math, will require cooperation by all team members.

Sharing Passions

I have found no better way to reveal myself to new students than to share one of my passions with them on the first day of school. *Passions*, in my sense of the word, are interests, hobbies, activities, and collections that are at the center of one's being. They are the essence of the soul. They are the things that raise blood pressure and get the adrenalin flowing—although some, such as music, sewing, writing poetry, or needlework, can slow the heartbeat and provide relaxation. They motivate and gladden the heart. Most delightfully of all, no two people's passions are exactly the same, and so the sharing of them is quite personal, very illuminating, and always intriguing.

This year, I plan to begin by sharing my hand puppet collection. We will all sit on the rug again. I will take each puppet out of a box and place it on my hand, and tell how and where it was acquired, demonstrate the voice I have given it, and explain how it has been used in past years, perhaps in plays or as a teacher's helper. Some have gone on vacations with students, and a few have even kept children company in the hospital or comforted them during sad and painful times. I will not pass the puppets around the group at this time because I want the children to remain focused on each puppet's history as it's told. When I have finished answering the children's questions, I will show them where the puppets will be kept and tell them how and when they may be borrowed or used in an activity center.

About once a month, I will introduce another passion in much the same way. Children are frequently reminded to share their passions, and a special table is provided for display purposes. Many children have invited their parents or other family members to the classroom to share their passions. I am not aware of any teachers' guide or in-service class on the subject of passions, but it is one of our favorite and most productive learning activities. Obviously, it is an excellent self-esteem booster.

◆ The Staff Can Share Passions Too

Recently, the staff at our school decided to use the entryway display case as a passions focal point for the entire school to view. Almost all the staff members participated in displaying their hobbies for one week at a time. We saw everything from African dolls to flutes from around the world to antique doll dishes to crocheting to mountain-climbing paraphernalia, during those three months of the project. In the end, we all knew each other better and school morale was at an all-time high.

Over the years, acquaintances who are aware of my many collections have supplied our class with thousands of seashells, buttons, colorful rocks, and bits of driftwood. The rare child who seems to have no passions of his or her own may start a collection from these stockpiles, and in no time is on the way.

Passions may not be things that can be placed on a table, or may be too large to be brought to school. Children have given karate or gymnastics demonstrations, ballet and tap dances, instrumental music performances, readings, slide shows of vacations, and many other nondisplayable passions. One child's passion led to an unforgettable field trip to his grandfather's farm so we could all see the pony he so expertly rode every weekend. His eyes shone as he accompanied each classmate around the corral on the back of his stalwart and patient friend. This child was wheelchair-bound at all other times.

◆ Other Collectibles

I have collected message buttons for years and now have more than 100. I wear one almost every day and the children look forward to reading them. This is one more way to make the printed word visible. It is also a fun hobby. There are many ways to discover or uncover a child's interests. Show-and-Tell is not the only way, and may be quite difficult, if not impossible, for some students who are reluctant to speak before the entire class. Children can express their interests through art, drama, music, creative movement, writing, free play, role play, and intimate conversations with you or other trusted classmates. For clues, listen to and watch your students closely.

Once you have seen a spark in a child, you have the privilege and the responsibility of nurturing that interest. You will do some of your finest and most rewarding mentoring once you have discovered a child's passions.

The First Assignment

Dismiss the children to their desks and give your first assignment. At this time, you are setting the standards by which most ensuing assignments will be handled, so of course you have decided ahead of time how you will proceed. My first seat assignment is usually a writing activity of some sort. The age of the children will be your guide. You may want to have them do a handwriting, spelling, math, or other curriculum area task. For instance, you might introduce a format on how and where to write names, dates, and other information. This format should be specific and consistent throughout the year.

Turning in Work

The way in which work is turned in will vary depending on the type of assignment. Some papers may be placed in a basket marked "FINISHED," if you are not going from desk to desk to monitor and give instant feedback. Sometimes it is appropriate to have children bring their completed papers directly to you for checking and conferencing while you are at the reading table. Papers in the FINISHED basket are checked within a day's time and returned to the students. Your paper passer can help redistribute graded work. Each child may also keep a folder in his or her desk in which to place all finished work. You can gather these folders at the end of each day, grade the papers, record the grades and comments on a record sheet in the folder, and return it to the child the next day.

Music and Gym Procedures

You will know before school starts what the procedures for music and gym classes are. Briefly discuss them with your class. By now, you have a class that knows how to line up in an orderly fashion and walk down the hall quietly. A reminder should be all that is needed. If not, practice one more time—and then one *more* time!

Children usually need a centering activity after these activities to bring them back to a classroom mode. When they return to the classroom, you could keep the classroom lights off for a minute and have them sit quietly or put their heads on their desks until you turn the lights back on. This is one of the most difficult transitions for young children to make.

End-of-Day Activities

Review the Day

Call the children back to the rug for the last time today. Briefly review all the information you have given them and allow time for questions and concerns to be addressed. Your morning meeting will seem like it happened days ago.

Finish the Story

Recall the beginning and middle of the story you began this morning. Allow some children to reiterate their predictions and then finish with gusto.

Papers to Go Home

During the first few days, you will be sending many informational papers and forms to parents via the children. Many documents have to be filled out by parents and returned to school. There are many headaches involved with this process: lost papers, papers eaten by the dog or little brothers, "I never got one of those," and "Mom lost it!" Always have a few spares and just keep trying.

Start saving plastic bags from the grocery store. They are the best totes for sending home papers, especially on the days you have children clean out their desks—and you are recycling, too! You will be sending home everything from supply lists to government attendance forms. Remember to send your own personal notes to families with that little pizzazz symbol affixed. The mail carrier is not the only disseminator of junk mail—many times there is such a profusion of paper, it's no wonder parents often do not read everything that their children bring into the house.

Keeping track of forms that must be filled out, signed, and returned by parents is easier if you attach a blank class list to a large envelope for each type and check off each child's name as the papers come in. This is a good job for an adult volunteer during the first few days.

Children usually like to know what these papers are about, so give them a brief explanation of each as you hand them around. You can distinguish the ones that need to be returned by starring them with a red marker.

◆ Model Expected Behaviors

During the first week, I always spend part of one afternoon with my students, role-playing the many ways children take their notes and school papers home. First, I am the *irresponsible* student, skipping gleefully into the house, throwing my jacket and lunch box in one direction, my books in another, and my notes and papers in the trash. "Hi, Mom! Goodbye, Mom! I'm goin' out to play!" This always brings riots of laughter. Then I play the *responsible* child, carefully putting away my jacket, setting my lunchbox on an imaginary countertop, and handing my papers to my mother, father, or caretaker. "Mom, these are VERY IMPORTANT PAPERS. You need to read and sign this one so I can take it back to my teacher tomorrow. Could you please do that before I go out to play? Thanks, Mom! And I want you to see how well I did in math today. Maybe you could tape this one to the fridge. I'm very proud of it!" Then I let the children play all of the parts in these little dialogs. The return rate of important papers improves quickly. I review this procedure again during the year if the return rate falls.

Role-playing is very effective for many learning situations. Don't be afraid to ham it up. The children love it and it is another form of bonding for teachers and children.

Bait for Tomorrow and Farewell

Frequently give children a hint of "Coming Attractions at a Classroom Near You!!!" I keep a small place on a bulletin board with that title and put up a word or picture to tantalize my students. Tomorrow will be exciting and different, so give them a clue about an upcoming event in the class. Try placing an object pertinent to one of tomorrow's lessons in a sealed mystery box to be passed around the group before you dismiss class for the day. Or you might tell them, "Tomorrow we will be learning about something that starts with the letter T," but don't give them the rest of the word! Children love intrigue. There are countless ways to ritualize the ending of the day, so find one that suits you and your students. Some teachers culminate the day with a song, poem, or other group activity. Others pose a question of the day that children must respond to before leaving; "Tell me one new thing you learned today." "Who was your friend today?" "Name one person in the story we read today." Children thrive on order and continuity and need beginnings and endings in their daily routines. Wish them goodbye in your own way and then go looking for a soft chair and a little adult company. By now, you deserve it!

A TYPICAL PRIMARY SCHEDULE	
8:00–8:15	Attendance, lunch survey, collection of parent papers, money collection, Pledge of Allegiance
8:15–8:30	Presentation of morning activities, explanations of centers and seat assignments
8:30–9:00	Reading group I/Centers/Seating assignments
9:00–9:30	Whole-group instruction/Spelling/Language arts
9:30–10:00	Reading group II/Centers/Seatwork assignments
10:00–10:30	Reading group III/Centers/Seatwork assignments
10:30–10:45	Recess
10:45–11:00	Assess center activity progress
11:00–11:30	Whole-group instruction/Writing/Handwriting
11:30–12:15	Lunch
12:15–12:30	Story
12:30–1:00	Whole-group math instruction
1:00–1:30	Individual math groups/Centers
1:30–2:00	Music/P.E.
2:00–2:30	Whole-group social studies, science, health, art
2:30–2:45	Finish story and closure activities (don't forget the bait!)

Fig. 3.1. Consult your district's curriculum guides for more details on the schedules you will be expected to follow.

Conclusion

Overplanning is the key to a smooth and organized beginning to every year in the classroom. Nothing can throw you off balance like a few minutes of "what do I do next?" Children instinctively take advantage of these unstructured moments to test the waters and try a little playground behavior in the classroom. These moments are confusing for them, as they are not sure what is expected. It is far better to end each day with unfinished tasks than to run out of gas an hour before the children go home. Try keeping a folder handy of short but structured activities to fill in any gaps you encounter. Teachers' guides for each instructional area have wonderful and productive ideas for enriching your program. Read beyond each day's lessons to find the projects you could use to fill each moment with excitement. Keep your students immersed in meaningful activities and you will be well on your way to a successful year.

Resources

(Note: The asterisk [*] denotes titles I believe are most helpful to first year teachers.)

*Albert, Linda. *A Teacher's Guide to Cooperative Discipline*. Circle Pines, Minn.: American Guidance Service, 1989.

*Barchers, Suzanne I. *Creating and Managing the Literate Classroom*. Englewood, Colo.: Teacher Ideas Press, 1990.

Barton, Bob. *Tell Me Another*. Markham, Ontario: Pembroke Publishers, 1986.

*Canter, Lee, and Marlene Canter. *Assertive Discipline*. Santa Monica, Calif.: Lee Canter and Associates, 1976.

Chernow, Fred B., and Carol Chernow. *Classroom Discipline and Control: 101 Practical Techniques*. West Nyack, N.Y.: Parker, 1981.

*Colorosa, Barbara. *Discipline: Winning at Teaching*. Boulder, Colo.: Media for Kids, 1983.

Curwin, Richard L., and Allen N. Mendler. *Discipline with Dignity*. Alexandria, Va.: Association for Supervision and Curriculum Development, 1988.

Discipline in the Classroom: Solving the Teaching Puzzle. Reston, Va.: Reston, 1979.

Ernst, Ken. *Games Students Play*. Millbrae, Calif.: Celestial Arts, 1972.

*Glasser, William. *Control Theory in the Classroom*. New York: Harper & Row, 1986.

Kinghorn, Harriet R., and Mary Helen Pelton. *Every Child a Storyteller*. Englewood, Colo.: Teacher Ideas Press, 1991.

Kruise, Carol Sue. *Learning Through Literature*. Englewood, Colo.: Teacher Ideas Press, 1990.

Madsen, Sheila, and Bette Gould. *The Teacher's Book of Lists*. Glenview, Ill.: Good Year Books, 1979.

Mamchak, P. Susan, and Steven R. Mamchak. *Teacher's Communications Resource Book*. Englewood Cliffs, N.J.: Prentice-Hall, 1986.

McManus, Mick. *Troublesome Behaviour in the Classroom*. Routledge, England: Nichols, 1989.

*Nelson, Pat. *Magic Minutes: Quick Read-Alouds for Every Day*. Englewood, Colo.: Libraries Unlimited, 1993.

Ryan, Kevin, and James M. Cooper. *Those Who Can, Teach.* Boston, Mass.: Houghton Mifflin, 1972.

*Trelease, Jim, ed. *Hey! Listen to This: Stories to Read Aloud.* New York: Penguin Books, 1992.

———. *The New Read-Aloud Handbook.* New York: Penguin Books, 1989.

Wallen, Carl J. *Effective Classroom Management.* Boston, Mass.: Allyn & Bacon, 1978.

Watkins, Kathleen Pullan, and Lucius Durant, Jr. *Complete Early Childhood Behavior Management Guide.* West Nyack, N.Y.: Center for Applied Research in Education, 1992.

4
Getting to Know Your Students

During the first few weeks of the school year, set aside a few minutes each day for a "Getting to Know You" activity. Through these activities you will build children's trust in you and each other. You and your students will soon find a heightened comfort level and sense of belonging, and friendships will develop more quickly. A spirit of unity or family will develop as you guide the children to discovery and expression of their inner selves.

In this chapter, you will find many activities to explore with your students. Some are "quickies," whereas others require moderate preparation and set-up time. Experiment with your own variations and browse through the Resources section at the end of this chapter for suggested readings and resources to help you expand your repertoire in this area, so crucial to the successful teacher.

Ways to Get to Know Your Students

Name Mural

Cut a large sheet of poster board into the appropriate number of pieces, jigsaw-puzzle style. Give each child a piece on which to write his or her name, and then have them decorate their pieces in their own way (fig. 4.1, p. 62). Reassemble the puzzle and display in a prominent place, perhaps over the entrance to the classroom.

Autograph Board

Lay out a large sheet of butcher paper and have the children "sign in" as they enter the classroom one morning. Draw geometric shapes around the names. During free time, each child can return to the paper and decorate the area around his or her name using crayons and markers.

Fig. 4.1. A name mural.

Classroom Tree

On a bulletin board or door, put up a tree with branches but no leaves. Have the children trace around their hands. Write their first names on the left hands and last names on the right ones. Children cut out their hand shapes and place them on the tree branches for leaves (fig. 4.2). Fall or spring leaf colors of construction paper guarantee a beautiful and personalized focal point for your classroom.

Fig. 4.2. A classroom tree.

Laundry Line

Give each child a T-shirt-shaped piece of white construction paper. Have them write their names on the shirts in bold letters of their own design, and then decorate their T-shirts with markers and crayons. Run a stout string across the room near the ceiling and put up the T-shirts with little plastic clothespins from the discount store.

Shaving Cream Writing

This is a fun and functional way to learn names and clean desktops at the same time. At the end of a week, go to each child's desk and write his or her initials on the desktop with inexpensive shaving cream. Then children smear the cream around to create a smooth layer in which they can write or draw with the tip of a finger or pencil eraser. You can use this opportunity to have your students practice a little handwriting or even a spelling list. Children can pair up and play tic-tac-toe at each other's desks or draw pictures of each other. When you've all had enough fun, pass out wet and dry paper towels to finish the cleanup. Your room will smell wonderful.

Magazine Picture Mural

Pass out old homemaking magazines and have children browse until they find three pictures that tell something meaningful about themselves. They might cut out pictures of favorite foods, clothes, a child playing, a grandparent, flowers, or even words. Provide a large sheet of poster board and a glue stick. During free time, children glue their triad of pictures in a group somewhere on the mural. At the end of the day, call for a class meeting to discuss what the selected pictures mean to them. Everyone will learn something new about their classmates and you.

Listen and Draw

This is a good activity for getting children to talk to each other in a way that requires them to work hard on communication skills. Divide the class into pairs. Give one child a slip of drawing paper and a pencil, and the other child one of the graphics shown in figure 4.3 or one of your own design. Adjust the level of difficulty depending on the age of your students. The children sit back-to-back. The child with the figure tries to describe how to draw it, as the partner follows instructions. Set a time limit of two or three minutes for each attempt. Then have the children switch tasks.

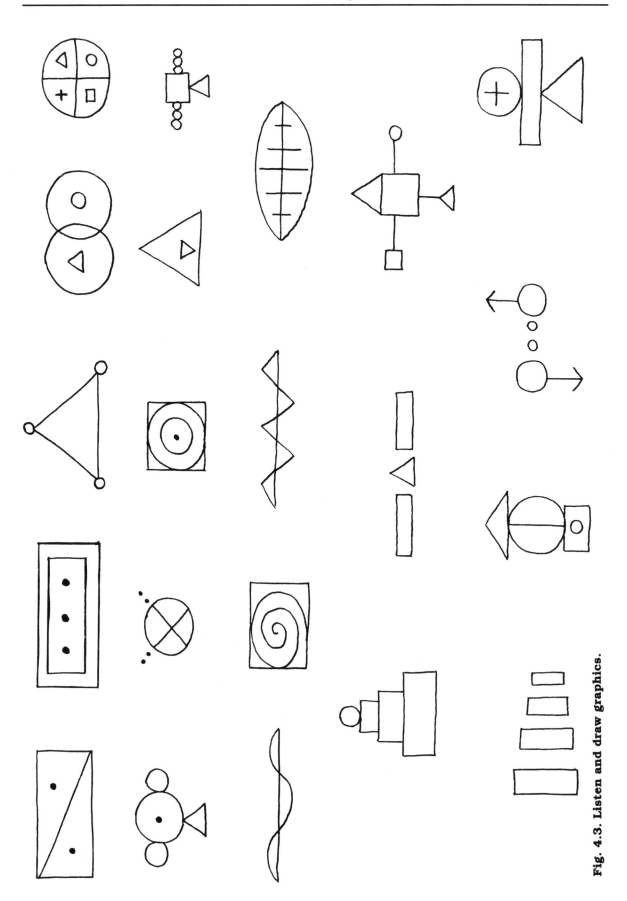

Fig. 4.3. Listen and draw graphics.

Scrambled Names

Before school starts one morning, take your class list to the chalkboard and write all of the children's names, but *scramble* the letters. For example, "Steven" becomes "eSevtn." After the day begins, ask the children to look for their names on the board. As the children find their names, ask them to go to the board and rewrite the names in the proper order. Your students have now had one more activity that matches names with faces and you have taken attendance without calling the roll.

My Head Is Full of Ideas

Enlist the help of a parent or other volunteer to help you make silhouettes of each child's head in profile, using a filmstrip projector or overhead projector as the light source. Trace the child's profile onto posterboard and cut out. Give each child his or her profile and have them create a collage by pasting magazine pictures of items that represent their concept of themselves on their silhouettes (see fig. 4.4). One side could be designated for the "now" me and the other side for the "future" me. Then use the heads for group discussions, and finally display them around the entrance to your classroom or on any other suitable bulletin board. You might even hang them from the ceiling on yarn. These heads are also good Back-to-School Night conversation pieces.

Fig. 4.4. A "head-full" of ideas collage.

Name Squares

Duplicate a grid like the one in figure 4.5, leaving enough spaces so every child can fill in his or her name at the top. The children must try to fill in each square with the name of an item that begins with the appropriate letter. Choose categories of special interest to your students. You may give the children one point for each square completed.

My name is	B	A	R	T
FRUIT	bananas	apples		tangerines
ANIMAL	bat	ape	rat	turtle
CARTOON	Bart Simpson	Alf		Tom and Jerry
COLOR	brown		red	

Fig. 4.5. A name square.

Circle Name Game

Assemble children into a close, seated circle. Say your name and pass an imaginary object to the person on your left. "My name is Mr. Jones and I'm handing you a baby elephant." Dramatize how heavy and large the elephant is as you pass it on. Encourage the children to fully use their imaginations during this activity as they think of their own objects and the body language needed to pass the object on (fig. 4.6). "My name is Billy and I'm handing you a porcupine!"

Fig. 4.6. Imaginary object passing.

Name Game Bingo

Create a grid with as many squares as members of your class—don't forget yourself! Fill in the blank grid randomly by putting all names on slips of paper; toss the names in a paper bag, draw out one at a time, and write it in a blank square. Then put all the names back in the bag. Give each child a grid and ample markers. Lima beans make inexpensive markers, and small squares of colored paper cost even less. Choose a child to be the caller and have the caller pull one name at a time out of the bag. The person named stands up briefly as everyone covers that name on the grid with a marker. The usual rules of bingo apply for trying to fill a row diagonally, horizontally, or vertically. The winner may be the next caller. This is a good first-week-of-school game; it will help children to quickly learn each other's names.

Find Someone Who

This is a game for children who can already read pretty well. Pass out a questionnaire something like the one below. Set a specific time allowance, about ten minutes. The children circulate around the room trying to find the right people to sign their names beside a true statement about themselves. A child may sign a classmate's questionnaire only once, so they need to talk to everyone to complete the task. When the time is up, call everyone to a class meeting and discuss the activity.

FIND SOMEONE WHO:

1. is wearing brown shoes

2. lives within two blocks of your home

3. has freckles

4. has the same birth month as I do

5. doesn't like ice cream

6. has broken a bone

7. has been to Disneyland

8. lives with Grandma

9. can whistle (prove it!)

10. can say all the words to "Hey Diddle Diddle"

11. can name the President of the United States

12. has more than three pets at home

13. likes spinach

Stand-Sit-Stand

This is a good activity for a day when the children have been working at their seats for a long time and need a little activity. Arrange chairs in a circle or have children remain at their desks. Begin the activity with children in a standing position. Ask children to show how they would stand back up if they were to sit on the following items:

Fig. 4.7. Stand-Sit-Stand game.

A PILLOW . . . . (stand up)

A CACTUS . . . . (stand up)

A CLOUD . . . . (stand up)

A BALLOON . . . . (stand up)

A ROTTEN TOMATO . . . . (stand up)

A THUMBTACK . . . . (stand up)

A DUCK . . . . (stand up)

A PORCUPINE . . . . (stand up)

A PAN OF HOT WATER . . . . (stand up)

A PAN OF COLD WATER . . . . (stand up)

A WAD OF BUBBLE GUM . . . . (stand up)

A PILE OF ROCKS . . . . (stand up)

A PILE OF FEATHERS . . . . (stand up)

A BASKETBALL . . . . (stand up)

A GOB OF PEANUT BUTTER . . . . (stand up)

A SKUNK . . . . (stand up)

THEIR SCHOOL DESK . . . . (stay seated)

Spider Web Game

Everyone gets involved when you use a ball of yarn to create a room-sized spider web. The possibilities are endless. The game begins as you say your name and, holding tight to the end of the yarn, toss the yarn ball to another person. The receiver then says his or her name, holds a portion of the yarn, and tosses the ball to someone else. Variations could include saying your name and your favorite toy, sport, color, food, TV show, game, animal, school subject, or relative. The yarn is easily rewound by playing the game in reverse, rewinding as you go. This is also a fun way to practice math facts: 2 + 3 = (toss the yarn). The catcher gives the answer and makes up a new problem. Or, announce a spelling word to the class. Each catcher gives the next letter of the word: **H** - (toss) - **E** - (toss) - **L** - (toss) - **P**.

Musical Pairs

Cut sheets of 9-x-12-inch white construction paper in half on an interesting and crooked diagonal line, creating peaks and valleys on each half. Pencil an *X* on the back of each piece so that the children will draw only on the correct side. Have the children get out their crayons and markers, give a half sheet to each child, and instruct them all to listen to the music you are about to play. There should be no talking during this activity. The music you choose can be dreamy or lively or any combination you like, but should evoke feelings, and should last about ten minutes. The object is to have children draw their impressions of the music they are hearing on their papers. Also encourage them to incorporate borders on their drawings. When they have finished, they go around the room looking for the person who has the other half of their sheet of paper. The two children put their papers together with tape to reform one sheet. They talk to each other about their drawings and what about the music made them draw what they did. Follow with a whole-class discussion of the activity during which each pair presents their art and their ideas. Without exception I have seen this activity encourage children to chat with each other openly, even the shy or reluctant ones. My students always ask to repeat this activity and love to bring their own music to share with the class. I have also used Musical Pairs as an ice-breaker for adult classes and back-to-school faculty meetings with great success.

Can We Talk?

Primary-age children love to just sit around and talk, and many may not often be heard by adults outside of your classroom. Periodically open the floor to discussion with topics like these:

If you had one wish what would you wish for?

My favorite time of the year is . . .

The best thing about last weekend was . . .

A person I would like to know is . . .

When I want to be alone I go to . . .

If I could be someone else, I would be . . .

I think I am really good at . . .

One thing I would like to change about me is . . .

The thing I would like to change about this school is . . .

Something that really worries me is . . .

The saddest thing that ever happened to me was . . .

If I were a grown-up I would/wouldn't . . .

I am afraid to/of . . .

Something that makes me laugh is . . .

Something that makes me cry is . . .

I wish teachers would never/always . . .

Remember, with activities like this, everyone has the right to pass. As the year goes by, children will become more comfortable about sharing their innermost feelings with the group. Never press a child for an answer.

The Mystery Circle

Have children bring mystery objects to school in paper bags. The class sits in a circle and one child sits in the middle, blindfolded. The "show-and-tell" child takes the mystery object out of the bag and passes it around the circle. Each child tells one small detail about the object to the blindfolded child in the middle, such as size, shape, color, use, and so on, until the item is guessed.

The Copycat Circle

Seat everyone in a circle. You start the first movement or sound, such as clapping your hands in a rhythm. The child to your left copies you as soon as she gets the rhythm, and then the child to her left joins in, and so on until everyone in the circle is clapping. When the clapping gets back to you, the child to your left begins a new movement or sound and passes it on around the circle. Some suggestions are: toe tapping, hand raising, whistling, snapping fingers, snorts, grunts, hums, and so on. This game gets pretty funny and usually ends up with a lot of laughter—good for the end of the day on Friday!

Are You My Popcorn?

Sometime during the first two weeks, bring in a sufficient quantity of popcorn for every child to have two large handfuls. Gather the children in a circle on the floor, spread out a plastic tablecloth in the center, and dump the popcorn. Each child searches for a unique piece of popcorn, takes it from the pile, and studies it closely for one minute while you remove the remaining popcorn and tablecloth. During this time, there should be no talking.

After the one-minute study period, have the children put their popcorn pieces back on a paper plate. Gently mix them a little. Now the fun begins. The children must retrieve their own special pieces of popcorn and then take turns telling how they knew which one was theirs: its characteristics, size, bumps, and so forth.

This activity is low-risk and gets everyone involved. After the discussion, bring back the tablecloth full of popcorn and enjoy eating the remainder. You could do this activity again and again using oranges, strawberries, peanuts in the shell, or homemade cookies. Your children will become very sophisticated observers of small details and will speak more articulately of their objects each time the activity is repeated.

The Shoe Garden

Create an unusual and very personal classroom garden on a window ledge, if you have one, or on a table with an ultraviolet lamp to provide light. Everyone in the class brings in one old shoe or boot, even you. The children fill the shoes about halfway with potting soil, a sprinkling of grass seed, and a top layer of soil. If it is springtime, get a flat of marigolds or petunias and put one in each shoe with the grass seed. Arrange the shoe garden to suit your fancy. Children enjoy the daily task of watering their shoes and waiting for the grass to grow. Eventually the grass will need a haircut, which is great fun for all. Each child can write or tell a little story about his or her shoe (where it has been, what it has seen, etc.). Gluing a pair of large, plastic google eyes from the craft store to the front of the shoes makes them even more interesting and amusing. My students like to name their shoe people.

Who in the World Am I?

Ask students to bring a few pictures of their favorite cartoon characters from comic books or TV guides. When you have enough for everyone, pin one to the back of each child, where the wearer cannot see it. The children form a circle and one child at a time goes to the middle. He asks questions of the children in the circle to try and figure out who he is. Variations of this game include using pictures of fairy-tale characters from a coloring book, making pictures of characters from some of your class literature, or making and enlarging prints of the childrens' class pictures on the copying machine.

Guess Who?

Have all the children but one put their heads down on their desks. The remaining child describes one characteristic at a time about one of the other children until someone is able to guess correctly who is being described. Then it is that child's turn to describe someone else. This is a good game to use right after an active period such as recess or gym. It gets everyone refocused and settled back into a quiet mode.

Ladybug! Ladybug!

Teach your class the old song:

> Ladybug, ladybug, fly away home,
> Your house in on fire - your children will burn!
> Except for the little one whose name is Ann,
> For she crept under the pudding pan.

Then have a circle discussion in which every child gets to tell about the two things in the home he or she would want to save if the house caught on fire. Emphasize that this is just a game and that if there were a real house fire, they should leave immediately without taking anything. Follow up with a ladybug drawing lesson and read a few of the excellent books for primary children on this subject. (Did you know ladybugs squirt "blood" from their knees when they are in danger?)

Conversation Quads

Ask for a paper-passer volunteer. Have her hand out 9-x-12 sheets of copy or ditto paper, one to each classmate. Show the class how to fold the paper in half, and then in half again to create boxes. Number the corners of the boxes, 1, 2, 3, and 4. "In box number 1, make a circle and fill it in with your favorite color. In box number 2, draw and color your favorite food. In box number 3, draw something that scares you. In box number 4, draw something you wish you had." Use these quads for discussion now or later in the day.

Moo! Moo! Where Are You?

This is a fun game for getting the giggles going. It is best played on the playground or in the gym, but can be done in the classroom as well. It can be used to divide the class into cooperative learning groups or just for fun. Into each child's ear, whisper the name of a farm animal (e.g., cow, pig, cat, dog, duck, chicken, lamb, etc.). Select only enough animals so that you have at least three children in each group. At your signal, all of the children begin to make their animal's particular sound and begin to move around, trying to find others who belong to their clan. When a completed group is formed, those children raise their hands or sit down to signal that they have accomplished the task.

Creating a Sense of Community: Class Mascots

The time invested in working with your students to create a sense of community will proportionately enrich and enhance every other aspect of your educational program. Many primary teachers bring a few stuffed animals to class and encourage their students to select one or two as class mascots. The children occasionally name the animals and sometimes take them home. This procedure can become a reverse "show-and-tell," and children truly enjoy taking a "class member" home for the night. Families sense a unique bonding between home and school when very special guests are brought home and shared.

Joseph Fred Washington

While we are on the topic of class mascots, I want to tell you about Joseph. He has been one of the best things that ever happened to my students and me. One day, about five years ago, one of my little second-graders came sobbing to me after recess. It took several minutes of tears and shoulder heaves before she was able to tell me her problem. When she was able to talk, she told me how a child from another class had hurt her with a particularly cruel racial slur. Because it was her first encounter of this kind, it was especially devastating. My heart broke for her. She was the only minority child in the primary wing of our school that year and an only child as well. I consoled her in the best way I knew how, but my hugs and words were obviously not going to be enough. She was terrified about going back to the playground again and wasn't able to identify the child who had hurt her so deeply. All our teachers talked with their students that day about the incident, but I had a very damaged little girl in my room who no longer saw school as a safe, happy place away from home.

Fate or divine intervention? I will never be sure! My husband and I went to a shopping mall that evening with no special purchases in mind. Our goal was just an evening of strolling and window shopping. As usual, I was drawn to a toy store to see the latest competition for kids' attention. I was browsing in the doll aisle and there he was! Joseph—a life-size, very realistic, beautiful black baby doll. My mind instantly did a replay of that morning's tragic playground incident, and I knew that, somehow, this adorable baby was going to help me heal little Myla's wounds. On the way home that evening, the plan took shape in my imagination. We stopped at another shop and purchased booties, a sleeper, a baby bottle, and a soft, blue, baby blanket.

Later that evening, this note was written in a faltering hand:

> Dear Folks,
>
> This is the saddest night of my life. I am leaving my baby boy with you. I cannot take care of him anymore. I hope you will find a good home for him. He is a good baby and won't be much trouble. He will need some brothers and sisters. Please take good care of him. His name is Joseph. Hug him a lot for me.
>
> Sincerely,
>
> Joseph's Mother

The first thing the next morning, I called a class meeting on the rug. I told the children that I had a very big problem and that I needed their help. Second-graders are fascinating little people. They are at an age between fantasy and reality and are reluctant to give up Santa Claus, the Easter Bunny, and the Tooth Fairy. I told them that a baby had been left in the back seat of my car at the shopping center the evening before, and that if I couldn't find him a good home, I would have to take him to the police. I read them the note and let them pass it around. They were totally caught up in the drama of the situation and clamoring with questions. I went to the classroom across the hall and brought Joseph back to my children. When I pulled the blanket away from his face, there were "oohs" and "aahs" of wonder from everyone. (He *is* very real-looking!) It was several seconds before the children began to catch on to my "fairy tale." I maintained the illusion and said how hard it would be to find a home with lots of brothers and sisters as his mother wished. I gently handed him to Myla and I will never forget the way her eyes widened and her face filled with adoration and love.

Fig. 4.8. Myla today.

Soon everyone was vying to take a turn holding him. As I continued to emphasize how badly he would need big brothers to teach him about being a "guy," the boys began to ask for their turn to hold the "baby."

A small miracle happened in our class that morning. A unanimous decision was made to adopt Joseph as our class child and to share in caring for him. Myla was the first to take him home for the night and became the person to decide which boy or girl would take him home every night thereafter. She kept him for us every weekend throughout that year. We kept track of Joseph's comings and goings that year and his diary became a journal of writing opportunities never found in teacher's guides.

Joseph was taken out to every recess, lunch, assembly, music, and P.E. class from that day on. He was in our school musical, complete with his own costume, and was also in our class picture.

Joseph still lives in our classroom, and his adoptive "family" is now in junior high school. They stop in to see him regularly. Joseph has now been to Canada, Disneyland, Disneyworld, and many places in between. He goes home with some child in our school every night and has the largest layette a child could ever have. His arms and legs are now sewn on with dental floss, someone pierced his ears, and someone else tried to trim his little fingernails. Other than that, he is in perfect condition. He has his own social calendar, and has been in well over 400 homes. Just this very morning, Joseph was late arriving at school, because he went to the funeral of the grandmother of the little girl who took him home last night. He has been reserved several months in advance for birthday parties. If Joseph could only talk, I could write a fascinating journal of the home lives of my students.

Myla, who is now a self-assured young lady, visits our classroom every so often. She remembers second grade and how she first encountered prejudice. But most of all, she remembers Joseph, and how he helped her survive a painful period in her life.

A Rabbit in the Classroom

For three years, my second-graders and I shared our classroom with another mascot, an enormous, silver-gray, French lop-eared rabbit named Merlin. With very little effort, Merlin was soon litterbox-trained and allowed to roam freely throughout the day. Because he was skittish about loud or sudden noises, my classroom was quieter for those three years than it had ever been before or since. Merlin's children spent many hours on the rug, reading quietly to him as his nose twitched in rhythm with their mellow voices. He often stretched himself across the top of a desk as "his" child did seatwork. Every afternoon, we could count on a little entertainment when Merlin, responding to some inner lagomorphic urge, would hop from one end of the room to the other, throwing in two or three athletic flips for good measure. He went out to recess everyday, sporting a bright blue puppy harness and leash. He especially loved tunneling in the sand pit. The child chosen to "hop the rabbit" each day was almost always someone who needed a little extra boost in self-esteem or responsibility.

I provided a folding wire cage for Merlin's confinement in the classroom at night and for children to take him home and care for him on weekends and holidays. Children shared the duties of food, water, and litterbox demands and were very thoughtful about bringing him fresh greens from home. Merlin had a big sweet tooth for jellybeans, especially the black and red ones.

Rabbits do love to chew on book bindings, bookshelves, and electrical cords, but can be dissuaded by applying rubbing liniment on these tempting delights. We finally provided a two-foot section of 2-x-4-foot wood, which Merlin lovingly dragged about the room or gnawed on contentedly for hours.

Other Classroom Pets

A living mascot is a very special way to create community spirit in the classroom. Animals take additional work on your part, but are well worth the effort if you are so inclined. Mice have lived in my classroom for years, in a thirty-gallon aquarium. They require very little attention and are quiet, reproductive to say the least, and a little stinky. They do best in a thick bed of white pine—not cedar—shavings, which needs to be cleaned once a week. Paper towel and toilet tissue rolls make wonderful nests and exercise mazes for small rodents. They eat just about anything and love fresh lettuce and carrot tops. The offspring may be taken home by any child who has a letter of permission from parents. I often trade in the latest litter for a bag of feed at the neighborhood pet store. Hamsters and gerbils are other good, easily contained choices for the beginning teacher who has a much larger job ahead than tending to pets.

◆ Box Turtles

Box turtles are also very rewarding, but you will need advice from a knowledgeable pet shop owner or veterinarian on their care. It is life-threatening for a box turtle to attempt to hibernate in the classroom through the winter. I learned this the hard way and have two such unfortunate creatures buried under third base on our playground. They need to be awakened every two weeks, watered, fed, and played with to keep them viable.

◆ And Still More Critters

An aquarium holding a few minimal-care fish, such as guppies or goldfish, is intriguing, educational, and very calming for children of any age. A terrarium can also be home to frogs, toads, newts, salamanders, and tree crabs. These creatures live in blissful harmony and eat mealworms, now available in most hardware stores, large drugstores, or wherever fishing supplies are sold.

Conclusion

During the first few weeks of school, become an avid kid-watcher. Note individual behaviors and what brings sparkles to their eyes. Using whole-group games allows you to observe children in social rather than academic settings and gives your students opportunities to get to know each other as well. Provide a classroom environment that promotes caring and sensitivity for others. When your room begins to feel like a home away from home for you and your children, you are well on your way to nurturing friendships, values, and memories that may well last a lifetime.

Resources

(Note: The asterisk [*] denotes titles I believe are most helpful to first year teachers.)

Andreas, Connirae, and Steve Andreas, eds. *Using Your Brain—for a Change*. Moab, Utah: Real People Press, 1985.

Anthony, Rose Marie. *Fun with Choral Speaking*. Englewood, Colo.: Teacher Ideas Press, 1990.

*Bagley, Michael T., and Karin K. Hess. *200 Ways of Using Imagery in the Classroom*. Unionville, N.Y.: Trillium Press, 1987.

Barrett, Katherine. *Animals in Action*. Berkeley, Calif.: Regents of the University of California, 1986.

*Borba, Michelle, and Craig Borba. *Self-Esteem: A Classroom Affair—101 Ways to Help Children Like Themselves*. San Francisco, Calif.: Harper & Row, 1978.

*Canfield, Jack, and Howard C. Wells. *100 Ways to Enhance Self-Concept in the Classroom*. Englewood Cliffs, N.J.: Prentice-Hall, 1976.

Carlin, Margaret F., Jeannine L. Laughlin, and Richard D. Saniga. *Understanding Abilities, Disabilities, and Capabilities: A Guide to Children's Literature*. Englewood, Colo.: Libraries Unlimited, 1991.

*Chenfeld, Mimi Brodsky. *Teaching Language Arts Creatively*. New York: Harcourt Brace Jovanovich, 1987.

Cihak, Mary K., and Barbara Jackson Heron. *Games Children Should Play: Sequential Lessons for Teaching Communication Skills in Grades K-6*. Glenview, Ill.: Good Year Books, 1980.

Comfort, Randy Lee. *Teaching the Unconventional Child*. Englewood, Colo.: Teacher Ideas Press, 1992.

Flugelman, A., ed. *New Game Book*. Garden City, N.Y.: Doubleday/Dolphin, 1976.

Gibbs, Jeanne, and Andre Allen. *Tribes—A Process for Peer Involvement*. Oakland, Calif.: Center-Source Publications, 1978.

*Ginott, Haim G. *Teacher and Child*. New York: Macmillan, 1972.

Green, Harriet Hope, and Sue Gillespie Martin. *Sprouts—Projects for Creative Growth in Children*. Carthage, Ill.: Good Apple, 1981.

Greenberg, Herbert M. *Teaching with Feeling*. Toronto, Canada: Macmillan, 1969.

*Hartline, Jo Ellen. *Me? A Curriculum for Teaching Self-Esteem in the Classroom*. Phoenix, Ariz.: Hartline Publications, 1982.

Hendricks, Gay, and James Fadiman, eds. *Transpersonal Education*. Englewood Cliffs, N.J.: Prentice-Hall, 1975.

Hill, Susan, and Tim Hill. *The Collaborative Classroom*. Portsmouth, N.H.: Heinemann Educational Books, 1990.

Holt, John. *How Children Learn*. New York: Pitman, 1967.

Johnson, David W., Roger T. Johnson, and Edythe Johnson Holubec. *Circles of Learning—Cooperation in the Classroom*. Edina, Minn.: Interaction Book Company, 1990.

Livo, Norma J., and Sandra A. Rietz. *Storytelling Activities*. Littleton, Colo.: Libraries Unlimited, 1987.

Matiella, Ana Consuelo. *The Multicultural Caterpillar: Children's Activities in Cultural Awareness*. Santa Cruz, Calif.: Network Publications, 1990.

McKay, Matthew, and Patrick Fanning. *Self-Esteem*. Oakland, Calif.: New Harbinger Publications, 1986.

*Mohr, Carolyn, Dorothy Nixon, and Shirley Vickers. *Books That Heal*. Englewood, Colo.: Teacher Ideas Press, 1991.

Ruckdashel, Candy. *Literature and the World Around Us—Integrating Literature into Basic Skills Programs.* Nashville, Tenn.: Incentive Publications, 1992.

Steinberg, Phil. *You and Your Pet—Aquarium Pets.* Minneapolis, Minn.: Lerner Publications, 1979.

———. *You and Your Pet—Terrarium Pets.* Minneapolis, Minn.: Lerner Publications, 1979.

Stock, Gregory. *The Kids' Book of Questions.* New York: Workman Publishing, 1988.

Thurston, Cheryl Miller. *What's in a Name?* Fort Collins, Colo.: Cottonwood Press, 1988.

Wayman, Joe, and Lorraine Plum. *Secrets & Surprises.* Carthage, Ill.: Good Apple, 1977.

5
Working with Parents

Getting to know your students and working with them is the lion's share of your job description, both during this first year and thereafter, but to be truly successful in teaching, it is imperative that you also find ways to establish a working relationship with parents. It is very important that you let parents know that you value their input about their children and that you are willing to work with them in designing mutually agreed-upon learning experiences for their child. Parents have the right to know what their child is being taught, how it will be taught, how discipline will be handled at school, when they can talk to you privately about their child, what they can do to help their child at home, how their child's work will be evaluated, and how they can help at school.

Many of these issues are usually clarified in a parent handbook issued by the school. They are further communicated through letters from you, during conferences, by classroom visitation during the school day, or at Open House or Back-to-School Night. Always keep your principal informed of your contacts with parents. My job description requires that I document all parent/teacher communications. It is a bother sometimes, but has been very helpful when questions arise. I think it is well worth the effort for a new teacher to keep a journal of all parent communications. Jotting notes in the margin of your lesson plan book is the easiest and most convenient way to do this, but you might also use a spiral notebook or telephone log solely for this purpose.

Class Newsletters

A monthly newsletter, written and published jointly by you and the children, is greatly appreciated by parents and is a good way to review what you have accomplished in the past month and what you will be teaching in the weeks ahead. Add a short biography of new students each month, too. Advertise for items you need for your next project and include a Help Wanted column. (See sample in fig. 5.1, p. 82.) There are many wonderful, copyright-free, reasonably priced, clip-art books in the art section of large bookstores. I also cut up old kindergarten workbooks and use the illustrations to punctuate family newsletters and other notes that go home with children. If you are computer-wise, there are several programs that will help you produce very professional-looking newsletters.

SECOND GRADE GAZETTE

The Mar. 1983

On Monday, March 14, we went to the Fine Arts Center and saw a play, "The UnWicked Witch." Thank you to Mrs. Jones and Mrs. Graham for helping us to get there!

* * * * * * * * * *

INTRODUCING OUR NEW STUDENT

LISA GEORGE
HAIR - BROWN
EYES - BROWN
PETS - Dog and cat
FAVORITE COLOR: BLACK
FAVORITE TV SHOW: THREE'S COMPANY

WELCOME LISA

JUNGLE BOOK IS FINISHED!

We are very proud of the book WE wrote this year. It is all about the jungle, the animals that live there, the food that is grown there and what it would be like to live there. We have learned so much and we hope that our parents will read it with us when we bring it home.

* * * * * * * * * * * *

Do you know what symmetry means?

We do!

Spike

Come in and meet our school bird. His name is Spike and he whistles at us. We hope he will learn to talk soon.

* * * * * * * * * * *

SILLY SOUP

We went shopping on March 9. We all bought vegetables and made soup. It was YUMMY!

* * * * * * * * * * *

We made kites out of pretty wallpaper and hung them in the front hall for the month of MARCH!

Fig. 5.1. Class Newsletter.

Report Cards

Standardized report or grade cards are a very sore spot for me, but you and I will most likely have to live with them for some time to come, so you may as well get to know the format and ideology as quickly as possible. They usually are accompanied by a brief explanation of the grading system used by your school or district and will be considered acceptable by the majority of parents as documentation of their child's progress or lack thereof. In the fall, I brainstorm with my students on the meaning of the grades they will earn. Together, we develop our own reporting system to supplement the district report card (see fig. 5.2, p. 84). I have had first-graders devise a pictorial version of a grade card that portrays subject areas in pictograph form, the grades being versions of extremely happy faces ranging downward to some very serious frowns. These "report cards" are filled in by the students, in conference with me, each grading period and are a meaningful part of our communication about the educational standing. Parents are delighted to be able to discuss this report with their child and feel it has more merit for the primary student than the usual version of grading. Second- and third-graders become much more discerning when designing their class report card and appreciate the opportunity to critique their own learning by conferencing with me. This is also their chance to let me know how I am doing—I have gotten a frown or two now and then. Keeps me on my toes.

Open Houses and Back-to-School Nights

Most elementary schools host a Back-to-School Night or Open House sometime during the first few weeks of school. The agendas for these programs vary greatly and your principal will inform you of your school's procedure. Many have a general, mass orientation meeting in the gym or resource center and then disperse parents to their children's classrooms. This may be the first and only time you meet many of your students' parents, so be well organized, concise, and make the most of this opportunity to communicate face-to-face. Depending on the amount of time allotted for this meeting, you may do a variety of activities. While parents are coming in, play a tape recording of your students singing songs that you have recorded in the past few days during their music classes.

1. Repeat the opening remarks you used on the first day of school.

2. Briefly outline your curriculum goals for the entire year.

3. Pass out a daily schedule and discuss it with the parents.

4. Give parents a tour of your classroom and explain how each area is used by the children.

5. If you have time and are so inclined, you could show a few slides or a video of your students at their various activities. A picture is still worth a thousand words.

NAME:	DATE:				
Reading:	Math:				
Writing:	Art:				
Spelling:	Science:				
Centers:	Social Studies:				
Working with others:	Other:				
How did I do?	Things I want to do next:				

I was terrific!   I could have done more   I didn't try

Fig. 5.2. Student/Teacher Report Card.

6. Direct parents to their child's desk, where the student has prepared a personal folder of items he or she would like them to see.

7. Most importantly, *relax!* The parents are just as anxious as you are. Offer them the same respect that you hope to get.

Open Houses Are Not for Conferences

RED LIGHT! RED ALERT! Quite often parents will try to corner and conference with you during an Open House. You will soon learn to diplomatically tell them that you would love to have the opportunity to talk with them at a more convenient time—"Would you like to set an appointment now?"

Open House Eyecatchers

The week before Open House, provide each child with a large sheet of white bulletin board paper. Divide children into pairs so that they can trace each other's bodies on the paper. For kindergartners, first-, and second-graders, it is helpful if you model the procedure of this activity. Have someone trace your outline, cut it out, and show various ways to draw in and color facial features, hair and clothing. When completed, the paper children can be seated at the children's desks (secured with tape), hands busily "working" on an assignment, ready to greet parents on the evening of Open House.

Another personalized desktop "student" can be made by having each child create a life-size self-portrait of his or her face on construction paper, trimmed and decorated with yarn or paper hair. Don't forget those freckles! Then the child traces and cuts out both hands. Have each child bring a wire coat hanger to school. Bend the coat hanger to create a stand for the face and hands, which will sit on the desk along with papers, books, or projects students would like to show their parents.

Children also enjoy decorating paper lunch sacks with crayons, markers, bits of yarn, and construction paper to create likenesses of themselves. Stuff the bags with recycling paper. Have each child bring in an old blouse or shirt, stuff it with wads of newspaper, insert the bag-head into the neck hole, and prop the "clone" at the student's desk. Older students may even want to create a full body by bringing in old jeans and a pair of sneakers. Walking into a classroom full of such "students" is quite a comical sight.

Put up a large sheet of butcher paper on the day of Open House and have each child draw a picture or write a message to parents. When the parents are in your room that evening, ask them to leave a message or drawing for their child for the next day. Write a message yourself to the children whose parents didn't come to the Open House. Tell them how special they are to you and how happy it makes you feel to have them in your class. Don't ever let any child feel like he or she is out there all alone on these special occasions.

During the first few weeks of school, you might set up a center filled with little boxes of all shapes, such as empty milk cartons, gelatin and pudding boxes, perfume boxes, cosmetic containers, small shoe boxes, and single-serving-size cereal boxes. Ask children to bring in a few to add to the collection. They will also need to bring in a couple of empty toilet paper tubes and fabric scraps. When they have a few free minutes, they can go to this center and make a miniature replica of their house or apartment building by covering the boxes in construction paper or fabric scraps, or by painting them with tempera to which you have added a few drops of liquid detergent so that the paint will adhere to the slick surfaces. Help them make windows, doors, chimneys, fire escapes, and other details that make their home unique. Provide circles of tissue paper, crepe paper, or fabric scraps for the children to stuff and fit into the ends of toilet paper rolls—these will become trees for the village they are creating. On Open House night, put the village on a table which you have covered with green butcher paper. Add a few meandering avenues and have the children label their houses. Or you can create a bulletin board by pinning the village to the board with corsage pins.

Parent-Student-Teacher Conferences

The first time you sit down to conference with the parents of your first students is sure to be an experience filled with varying degrees of apprehension. If you are in your early twenties, this may be your first time to speak to adults as an authority figure, and the parents of your students will be older and more experienced with children than you are. I think it is wise to acknowledge this, while keeping clearly in mind that you are the one with the teacher training and the responsibility for the daily educational progress of each child in your classroom.

As with your first year of teaching, your first conferencing experience will be more successful if you are extremely well organized and prepared in advance. The amount of time allotted and the purposes of conferences vary from school to school. You will be told about the guidelines by your principal or supervisor. I offer ideas that have worked well for me, as well as suggestions for conference forms that you may find helpful in structuring these initial meetings with parents.

If you sent an introductory letter before school started, met a few parents the first day of school, and had an Open House prior to conferences, you already know most of the children's families. Conference opportunities are the time to learn more intimate details about each student in a private setting.

Things to Do Before Conferences

1. Review each child's folder and make notes on details that have any significance to his or her current progress in school. Don't bring up old problems from past years, even if they have been documented by previous teachers, if they are no longer significant. *Do* note if a child seems to be losing ground in an area that was a past strength. You will want to seek the parents' insights regarding any such regression. Review test results, report cards, social history, and discipline records.

2. Consult with any other teachers who may also conference with a student's parents (special education, speech, Chapter, social worker, music, physical education). Occasionally, your principal may ask or be asked to sit in on a conference, particularly with a first-year teacher. Each member of a conferencing team should be aware of information that will be shared in advance. Prepare multiple copies of written reports to pass out to everyone.

3. Keep samples of children's work from each academic area. Include examples of areas of strength, as well as areas of concern, so you will be able to show parents exactly what you are referring to. Each child should be encouraged to help select these pieces.

4. Offer parents and their children the opportunity to meet with you jointly. Encourage the children to participate fully in all discussions.

5. Conference around a table or child's desk, never from behind your desk.

6. Make every effort to conference with *every* parent, even if it requires a home visit, a meeting at a coffee shop, or an evening or Saturday in the classroom. I have worked with families who, because of past difficulties, refused to risk running into the principal or other teachers and would not come to the school. If all else fails, conference over the telephone. Tell your principal what you are doing about these difficult situations.

◆ Pre-Conference Form

Send each parent an appointment and purpose notice at least one week, and preferably two, in advance of the conference. The form should provide space for the parents to write in a topic they would like to discuss, and an alternative time, if necessary. (See fig. 5.3, p. 88.) Confirm the conference with a written response (fig. 5.4) as soon as possible. As you can see, we are now getting into some of the endless paperwork that teachers are always bemoaning. It is a lot of work, but it is necessary and worth every bit of effort.

Date:

Dear Parents of _____,

I will be conferencing with all of my students' parents during the week of November 8–12. The purpose of this conference is for me to sit down for a few minutes with you and your child, in our classroom, and talk about how this school year is going and make any necessary changes for the future. I have set aside this time for your family:_____.

Miss Jones

****
(Please return this portion to me.)

Date: _____ Time: _____

Alternate date and time: _____

Parent signature: _____

I would like to discuss:

_____

_____

Return to Miss Jones

Fig. 5.3. Pre-conference notice form.

Parents of _____,

Thank you for confirming this conference time:

Date: _____ Time: _____.

Miss Jones

Fig. 5.4. Confirmation notice.

The Conference

Create a comfortable conferencing atmosphere that includes adequate informal seating for all participants and a cup of coffee or tea, if you are so inclined. Begin informally, perhaps by having the student show his or her parents a current project or work in progress. Point out the child's contribution to the classroom environment.

Always begin and end a conference with the most genuinely positive observations you can make about each child. Allow the parents and child time after each topic to respond and add their own comments. Webster's definition of a *conference* is "an interchange of views." So often, teachers dominate this precious little time together. Be prepared to hear over and over again, through the coming years, that "Johnny is having trouble in math because I was never a good student either. It runs in the family!" Make good eye contact; be a perceptive observer and an attentive listener. You will gain new insights into every child during these brief but valuable few minutes. Guard against using "edu-babble," technical language that is meaningless to parents. Many parents will be too embarrassed to ask for clarification of strange terms that have become so familiar among educators. Ask frequently if there are any questions.

◆ Conference Form

Follow some sort of conference plan. This will help you cover everything you intend to discuss and keep you all focused. Your school may have a standardized form. If not, you may want to use one similar to the one in figure 5.5, page 90.

Parent–Student–Teacher Conference

STUDENT _____ GRADE _____

PARENTS _____ DATE _____

TEACHER _____ OTHERS _____

AREAS OF STRENGTH:

AREAS OF CONCERN:

CHANGES IN HOME SITUATION:

REMARKS FROM TEACHER/SCHOOL:

REMARKS FROM STUDENT:

REMARKS FROM PARENT:

SUGGESTIONS FOR TEACHER/SCHOOL:

SUGGESTIONS FOR STUDENT:

SUGGESTIONS FOR PARENT:

FOLLOW-UP PLANS:

INFORMATION FROM OTHER STAFF MEMBERS:

Fig. 5.5. Conference form.

Parents Helping Their Children at Home

Many parents will ask you what they can do to help their children at home. Most are sincere in asking for your ideas. A few are merely going through the motions, acting as they think a concerned parent should, and do not follow through with your suggestions in spite of their good intentions. Over the years, I have gathered a wide variety of activities for parents and children that require minimal expense, are fun for everyone, and are not redundant of the learning experiences at school.

To Drill or Not to Drill

I do not recommend that children be asked to complete photocopied or mimeographed drill and practice worksheets or unfinished workbook pages at home. These literally become homeWORK for children, and parents as well. This type of repetition is counterproductive. Children resent doing this type of activity and parents become frustrated trying to enforce completion of such busywork, firm in the belief that they are helping their child to be a better student.

I feel children need "down time" after school to indulge in the important childhood business of imaginative play, developing social skills with siblings and friends, and engaging in "gross motor activities." But children should have a few minutes of guided interaction with their parents each day. These activities are discussed on the following pages.

Parents and Children Reading Together

It is a well-documented fact that time spent reading with, to, and by children, at home with a caring adult, is the one activity guaranteed to improve a child's performance at school. But telling most parents to read to their child or listen to their child read is not enough. You must carefully select materials from your class or school library that match the child's interests and abilities. To make this home reading program most effective, design a written home reading contract with the child, giving the page numbers to be read each day. Once I started individualizing home reading assignments, parents became much more involved with their children's home reading efforts. These weekly contracts are signed by me and the child before they are taken home, and signed by the parents before they are returned to school. The assigned pages never exceed what I feel that child can comfortably read in a ten-minute period. I also send home a chapter book that a parent can finish easily by reading to the child for ten minutes or less each day. Parents are very grateful for this structured type of homework. They know the expectations and are relieved to have materials that they can rely on for helping their children.

Alternative Parent/Child Activities

The materials for these activities can be produced jointly by parents and children from common household items. I usually present some of these activities, in booklet form, to families at a parent information evening where I show actual samples for each activity. (See the appendix for this booklet.) Other times I offer individual ideas to parents who ask for specific activities. These ideas have been family tested for several years and found valuable. I prefer to help families plan for home*fun* rather than home*work*. When children ask for additional home projects, you will know you are on the right track.

◆ The Jughead

Have parents prepare a clean, empty, one-gallon, plastic milk jug by drawing a face on the side opposite the handle with markers, and cutting out a three inch slice for a mouth. Periodically send home new lists of oversized sight words, math facts, and spelling words to be stored in this *Jughead*. Children love having Jughead spit out a few words or math problems to work on; they can then put them back in his mouth as they say or solve them. Parents like knowing exactly what their child is working on at school and having control over a simple drill and practice activity. For kindergartners, I send home colored strips of paper, letters of the alphabet, and numbers I want the children to work with at home. Later in the year they can add their first sight words to the collection.

◆ Wednesday Night Shaving Cream Fun

Show parents the shaving cream method for practicing writing or spelling words at home (see the appendix). I suggest that parents spend ten or fifteen minutes on spelling practice every Wednesday evening on the kitchen table after dinner. Spelling test scores always increase quickly when parents let children do this activity—and it cleans the table nicely as well! Young children enjoy writing their letters or numbers in shaving cream. The shaving cream table is a great place to practice addition and subtraction facts.

There are also some fun bathtub foams on the market that can be used in the same ways. Smear some foam on the tiles in the tub area and help little ones practice their alphabet or numbers while relaxing in a tub of warm water after a hard day at school. This short time of fun and intimacy cements new concepts very quickly.

◆ Lotion Slates

Another way to practice spelling, writing, or math is with a lotion slate. Put about six tablespoons of inexpensive hand lotion and a few drops of food coloring into a zip-lock plastic bag. Squish the ingredients around until mixed. Let any air out of the bag, seal, and smooth into a wonderful feeling and smelling slate. Children can write on this slate with a fingertip or the eraser end of a pencil. These slates are remarkably durable; I have a couple that have lasted in the classroom for two years of daily use. Practicing addition and subtraction facts is a lot more fun on a lotion slate.

◆ Play Dough Projects

Give parents a copy of the dough recipe from the appendix and ask them to help their children create objects for social studies, science, health, or other units of study, at home. Items they can create together might include animals for a shoe box diorama, planets, relief maps of their home state, play foods for a unit on the four food groups, or a set of teeth for a dental unit. The possibilities are limited only by what you are studying in school.

◆ Good Games for Families

Encourage parents to invest in a few good games from the toy store. Parents often ask for suggestions for educational games for birthday or holiday giving. The following games can be found currently in stores and have been field-tested and found worthy by me and my grandchildren. Many important skills are learned by playing these games, and they promote the family interaction and conversation so lacking in many homes these days. Also ask parents to provide educational computer games to balance the aggressive computer games so many children spend hours at during their free time.

Alphabet Land	memory games of all kinds
Alphabet Soup	Monopoly Jr.
ASAP the Quick Think Game	The Mother Goose Game
Bingo (of all kinds)	Outburst Jr.
CandyLand	Picture Picture
Chutes and Ladders	Scattergories Junior
Boggle Junior Letters	Scrabble for Juniors
Boggle Junior Numbers	Scrutineyes Junior
Crackers in my Bed	Sorry
Golden Sound Safari	Spellway
Hangman	Tri-Ominos
Hi Ho! Cherry-O!	Twenty Questions for Kids
Mickey Mouse Yahtzee	Where Are They?

◆ **Playing Store**

Children still love to play "Store." Ask parents to put price tags on a few food items and send their child shopping with the loose change they have around the house. This activity lends itself to all kinds of reading and math learning opportunities. Older children can look up real prices in the food section of the newspaper and even help create a shopping list or balance the weekly food budget. Get all of the spices out of the cupboard and have the child arrange them in alphabetical order.

◆ **Kitchen Activities**

Parents can also involve their children in cooking activities, even if it is only to read the directions for preparing microwave meals. Cleaning and preparing food is still a great activity for measuring, reading directions, learning sequencing, and increasing small motor control. Children can cut up sandwiches, pancakes, or waffles into squares and triangles, or learn more about fractions by cutting them into fourths, thirds, and eighths. Counting pizza slices is another opportunity to teach fractions in the kitchen. A small child can have fun drawing the family dinner table as seen from the viewpoint of the light overhead. Have him or her draw the place settings and all the serving bowls full of food while the parent is preparing the meal.

◆ **Calendar Activities**

Also ask parents to provide a calendar for their children so that they can keep track of their own daily activities, learn the months and days of the week, track special days and chores, and see the passage of time. Provide attractive stickers and colored markers so the child can mark the important days in his or her life. Send parents a copy of this old rhyme to teach children. I am finding that not many children or their parents know this little poem anymore:

> Thirty days hath September,
> April, June, and November,
> All the rest have thirty-one,
> Excepting February alone,
> And that has twenty-eight days clear,
> And twenty-nine in each leap year.

Start Your Own Resource File

Keep your ears to the ground and your eyes open for more ideas for parents to use with their children at home. Teaching magazines have wonderful ideas every month. Jot some of your favorites on index cards and start a home activity file for future use. Never hesitate to pick up new ideas from old teachers. Ask for their advice and report back to them whenever one of their ideas has helped you. Also, always let your principal and supervisor know what activities you are sending home. It is important that they be aware of all communications you have with parents. They will be most pleased that you are going this extra mile so soon in your career. If your school doesn't already have one, talk to your principal and librarian about the possibility of starting a *parent lending library*, incorporating some of the books suggested in the Resources section at the end of this chapter. The home-school connection is more important than it has ever been before and your efforts will not go unnoticed or unappreciated.

Conclusion

There is a growing movement across the country to get parents more involved with the educational process. In my experience, the more direction and actual materials I provide for families, the more response and involvement I get. Many parents are more than eager to help their children at home, but lack the ideas and methods. As mentioned, the pamphlet in the appendix at the end of this book may be photocopied and stapled together for use as a handout to parents. It is our task to give them these projects and direction and the feedback that encourages them to become active partners in education.

Resources

(Note: The asterisk [*] denotes titles I believe are most helpful to first year teachers.)

Baratta-Lorton, Mary. *Mathematics Their Way.* Menlo Park, Calif.: Doubleday/ Addison-Wesley, 1976.

*———. *Workjobs for Parents.* Menlo Park, Calif.: Addison-Wesley, 1975.

Baskwill, Jane. *Parents and Teachers—Partners in Learning.* New York: Scholastic, 1989.

Bennett, Steve, and Ruth Bennett. *365 TV-Free Activities You Can Do with Your Child.* Holbrook, Mass.: Bob Adams, 1991.

Berger, Eugenia H. *Beyond the Classroom.* St. Louis, Mo.: C. V. Mosby, 1983.

Boston Children's Medical Center. *What to Do When There's Nothing to Do.* New York: Dell, 1967.

Burnham, T. Lee. *The Home & School Connection: How Your Home Life Affects Your Child's Success at School.* Salt Lake City, Utah: Desert Book Company, 1986.

Collins, Myrtle T., and Dwayne R. Collins. *Survival Kit for Teachers (and Parents).* Glenview, Ill.: Good Year Books, 1980.

Engelmann, Siegfried, Phyllis Haddox, and Elaine Bruner. *Teach Your Child to Read.* New York: Simon & Schuster, 1983.

*Fredericks, Anthony D. *Involving Parents Through Children's Literature.* Englewood, Colo.: Teacher Ideas Press, 1990.

Kappelman, Murray, and Paul Ackerman. *Between Parent and School.* New York: Dial Press/James Wade, 1977.

Kroth, Roger L. *Communicating with Parents of Exceptional Children.* Denver, Colo.: Love Publishing, 1975.

Kyte, Kathy S. *In Charge—A Complete Handbook for Kids with Working Parents.* New York: Alfred A. Knopf, 1983.

*Maxted, Traci, and Melinda Swezey Tomsic. *Don't Just Bake Cookies: A Handbook to Creative Volunteering in the Elementary School.* Englewood, Colo.: Teacher Ideas Press, 1990.

Miller, Mary Susan, and Samm Sinclair Baker. *Straight Talk to Parents.* New York: Stein & Day, 1976.

The National PTA Talks to Parents. New York: Doubleday, 1989.

Robinson, Jeri. *Activities for Anyone, Anytime, Anywhere.* Boston: Little, Brown, 1983.

Simon, Sarina. *Amusing Ways to Develop Your Child's Thinking Skills and Creativity.* Los Angeles: Lowell House, 1989.

*Spaete, Susan. *Parent Programs & Open Houses.* Elgin, Ill.: Building Blocks Publications, 1987.

*Stenmark, Jean Kerr, Virginia Thompson, and Ruth Cossey. *Family Math.* Berkeley, Calif.: Regents of the University of California, 1986.

*Sullivan, Emilie P. *Starting with Books: An Activities Approach to Children's Literature.* Englewood, Colo.: Teacher Ideas Press, 1990.

Sutton-Smith, Brian, and Shirley Sutton-Smith. *How to Play with Your Children.* New York: Hawthorne Books, 1974.

*Vodola, Peter, and Connie Briggs. *Your Best Back-to-School Night Ever.* Brea, Calif.: Peanut Publications, 1987.

Young, Roger. *Learning to Read in the '90s—An Interactive Playbook.* Berkeley, Calif.: Celestial Arts, 1992.

Teaching Magazines

Arithmetic Teacher
1906 Association Drive
Reston, VA 22091

Childhood Education
Early Years: Teaching PreK-8
P.O. Box 912
Farmingdale, NY 11737-0001

Instructor
P.O. Box 6099
Duluth, MN 55806

Language Arts
National Council of Teachers
    of English
1111 Kenyon Road
Urbana, IL 61801

Learning
P.O. Box 51593
Boulder, CO 80321-1593

The Mailbox
The Education Center, Inc.
1410 Mill Street
P.O. Box 9753
Greensboro, NC 27499-0123

The Reading Teacher
800 Barksdale Road
P.O. Box 8139
Newark, DE 19714-8139

Science and Children
1742 Connecticut Avenue NW
Washington, DC 20009

6
Centers

Experience and inquiry centers, located strategically around the classroom, can provide the alternatives that ensure all children will be enticed into meaningful and beneficial learning activities, without requiring your physical presence and direction. When one part of your class is actively participating in an instructional activity with you, such as reading or math group, the rest of the children *will* be doing *something*—whether you have planned for it or not! For many new teachers, providing multiple and simultaneous activities is the most difficult challenge of the first year. Unfortunately, most publishers of the textbooks you will be using provide enough seatwork reproducibles to keep children at their seats, working like little drones, for hours every day. Fortunately, many textbook publishers have recently made great strides toward becoming more sensitive to the current learning styles of children and teaching styles of teachers. Textbook guides now contain many suggested lessons for teaching more wholistically, and contain fewer drill and practice exercises. Study your guides and manuals carefully and, using your knowledge and instincts, select alternative and appropriate "other" learning experiences for your students on a daily basis. Check out a few of the books suggested in the Resources section at the end of this chapter and scan teaching magazines for other good ideas.

The Purpose and Design of Centers

Appropriate and well-designed centers free you to concentrate your attention on small groups of children for specific teaching objectives. They encourage children to be more self-directing and to make choices in their own interest areas. Keeping *all* children purposely engaged *all* of the time is the best classroom management technique I can propose to you, and a good learning center is one place to do this. Good learning centers have these characteristics:

1. They promote independence in problem solving and creative thinking.

2. They contain a wide variety of materials related to one topic.

3. They stimulate imagination and active learning.

4. They can be used by all children, within a wide range of abilities.

5. They build on students' previous knowledge.

6. They provide active, hands-on learning experiences.

Centers may be organized in many ways, depending on their objectives and requirements for space and materials. Most centers will require an initial demonstration of procedures by you so that children understand what they are to do; how, when, and where to do it; what to do with completed projects; and how to participate in the evaluation and celebration process. Some centers are meant to be used by a group of children; others are used by one child at a time. Learning centers can be extensive, incorporating audiovisual equipment, science experimental equipment, and a wide array of library materials. A few are portable and are designed to be taken to a child's desk, or even home to be shared with the student's entire family. Some of the centers I suggest may not result in a finished product or written document, but are meant merely to pique the imagination or lead a child to a more penetrating, in-depth exploration of a topic.

Initially, it takes a great deal of your time to set up centers, but most teachers will tell you they are the mainstay of the classroom. In this chapter, I describe a few centers that have worked well for my students in the primary grades. As always, your creativity and particular circumstances will guide you to create the centers that work for you and your children.

Finding Spaces for Centers

Even a very small classroom can accommodate several centers in limited spaces. Have your building custodian save the large cardboard cartons toilet tissue comes in. Remove one side and the top for an instant center area. These boxes also make serviceable and portable study carrels for individual students. They can also be placed on a child's desk to help with distraction problems or to ensure privacy during testing. Sturdy cardboard boxes stacked one on the other also work well for centers. Old fold-up TV trays can hold small centers and provide extra work space for almost any activity. I found some old chart racks in a storeroom at our school and ran up two curtains to fit them. They are indispensable for creating study corners away from the distractions of other activities.

A Center for the First Weeks

Before the children arrive for the first day, I set up a table of goodies that will set the tone for science inquiry throughout the year. I title it "WHAT IN THE WORLD—?" Items to be found there might include a bird's nest, feathers, animal bones (chicken leftovers are a good starting source), a hornet's nest, briars and brambles, seed pods, rocks of different types and colors, nuts, bolts, and gears, shells of all kinds, magnets, a broken wristwatch, magnifying glasses, pieces of wood, intriguing spare car parts, dried gourds, and just about anything else I can get my hands on from Mother Nature. A large jar filled with soil and dead leaves is the ideal home for a dozen earthworms purchased cheaply at a bait shop or sporting goods section of a drugstore. A clear plastic container of mealworms also makes for lively conversation. Very soon the children themselves bring in more items than I know what to do with. My science lessons evolve from these curiosities and I never know where they will lead. Just follow the children's interests and you can't go wrong. A strong interest in some particular item can lead to the development of a more involved learning center later on in the year. It all depends on the children and your energy level.

Other Centers

The Body Center

One of the centers I set up during the first few weeks is a "Draw Your Body" area. The activities performed here kill many birds with one stone. There will be a lot of interaction between students as they help each other outline their bodies and add details. I use the finished bodies (at Open House, for example) and then display them on the walls outside our room. As the seasons change, I have the children make appropriate clothing or costumes for their "wall people." During our dental hygiene unit they will add toothy mouths, and as the children lose their baby teeth throughout the year, they blacken out the matching teeth on their wall people. On a student's birthday, the child will find his or her wall person wearing a paper crown. I have also outlined kindergartners on brown paper at Christmastime and turned them into gingerbread people with paper "peppermint" button eyes, candy-cane mouths, and a generous piping of white paint "frosting" around the edges. You will probably think of many more ways to enhance these bodies throughout the year.

Science Centers

Your first "WHAT IN THE WORLD—?" exhibit can evolve into a full-fledged science center in the first few weeks of class. This center will be ever-changing, as projects are conceived and executed, but like the other centers, remains a focal point of study for the current topic. Centers can be designed to enrich and expand every curriculum area: spelling, math, reading, science, health, social studies, art, and so on.

◆ Bones and Skeletons

Start saving the larger bones from your chicken dinners. Clean them by boiling them for a few minutes. Then soak them a while longer in a bowl of water with two tablespoons of bleach. Let them dry out and take them to school for a BONES science inquiry table. If you ask the children to do the same, you will soon have the makings for some very interesting projects. My students saved all the bones from their chicken school lunches and we built dinosaur skeletons (fondly called

"Finger-Lick-A-Sauruses") from them. I molded heads from clay, inserted raw rice for teeth, and provided picture wire to hold the bones together on a slab of Styrofoam or plywood.

The butcher at your grocery store will gladly provide you with some interesting larger bones for study at school. Have him slice a beef femur lengthwise, and you will have a wonderful example of marrow and a ball-and-socket type of bone to study with your students. Send away for a few owl pellets to continue your study. Check with your science supervisor for the nearest source.

◆ Instant Greenhouses

As part of a science unit, or just for curiosity's sake, set out self-closing plastic sandwich bags, a variety of seeds (edible sprout types make this even better), and paper towels. Children soak the toweling with a little water, sprinkle a few seeds on the towel, and seal the seeded towel in a plastic bag. The bags can be taken home, displayed on the bulletin board, or left near a window. Many kinds of experiments can be generated in this center. I once had a child who was positive that he could grow an alphabet noodle bush by planting one of the pasta letters in such a bag. Later that year, when his experiment had proven a miserable disappointment, we had a mom come in and teach the children to make homemade noodles. She used assorted cookie cutters to make the most wonderful noodles, bubbled in chicken broth, that we have ever eaten. So, Johnny, noodles are made, not grown, and thank you for trying it out. That is how good thinkers learn.

◆ The Dirty Potato and Other Lovely Molds

Bring in a big fat Idaho potato, peel it, and cut it into two pieces. After recess or lunch that day, ask children if they think their hands are fairly clean. I guarantee most of them will say, "Yes!" Ask them to pass around the first half of the potato and to rub their hands all over it. It will begin to look quite gross about halfway through the passing. Place this piece in a clean jar and close the jar. Then have the children wash their hands thoroughly with soap and water. Pass the second half of the potato around the class and have them rub this piece with their clean hands. Place this potato in another clean jar and seal that jar. In three or four days, the dirty potato will begin to grow a lovely little mold and germ garden. The clean potato will turn gray as it dries and disintegrates, but it will not grow mold. Eventually the dirty potato will be consumed by the molds and will turn to a slime that will surely impress your students with the importance of keeping their hands fairly clean.

Other mold gardens can be grown by placing bread, orange slices, apple chunks, cheeses, and other fruits and vegetables in resealable plastic bags. Leave them on the science table for a few days and have the children write down their observations.

The Writing Center

In our room, there is a one-armed, wooden desk with a storage area beneath the seat. Children may choose to sit in the writer's desk to work, or may take the materials they need to their own desks or another suitable work area.

Stored in one attractively covered cardboard box beneath the seat are pencils, pens, markers, rulers, and every other conceivable writing implement we can find. Another box contains upper- and lowercase alphabet rubber stamps, cartoon stamps, facial and body parts stamps, and a variety of colored ink pads. A third box contains a wide variety of papers—lined, unlined, colored, white, small and large sizes—plus envelopes of all types for mailing generated letters and notes. A fourth box contains suggestions and inspirations for writing, such as story starters, unfinished stories, CLOZE stories, comic strip blanks, provocative pictures to build stories around, and newspaper headlines.

Here are a few of our most successful story starters. They are printed on index cards and stored on a large, metal, library ring:

If I had three wishes, I would wish:
1. _____
2. _____
3. _____

One night, as I was falling asleep, I heard voices in my toy box. I opened the lid and . . .

If I ever become president (principal, teacher, mayor), I will do these three things:

One day I opened the refrigerator. There on the middle shelf sat a . . .

What do the hermit crabs talk about after we go home each day?

I woke up last night and there was a bright light shining in my window. I . . .

Last night I heard strange voices coming from my closet. I opened the door and . . .

Your whole family has turned into animals. Write a story about your new family. Don't forget to tell about yourself.

One day as I was riding the bus to school, it started to fly. We ended up in . . .

The television reported that a polar bear escaped from the zoo. You have just gone to bed and you hear a noise outside your bedroom window. And then . . .

I was walking in the woods one evening and I heard a loud noise behind me. I turned around and . . .

What would a bar of soap say to your hands right now?

Being a grown-up would be fun because I could . . .

I planted an eye from my old teddy bear in the garden last week. The next morning I noticed that something had begun to grow. It was . . .

Make up five rules for grown-ups.

A worm has a strange life because . . .

Your homework has been taken from the kitchen table. In its place is a piece of paper with a strange pawprint on it. I think . . .

I would like to be a garden snake for one day so I could . . .

You are playing on the beach one day and you find huge footprints in the wet sand. You follow them to a hollow tree and . . .

One day I discovered an old house. No one was living there. The door was open, so I went inside and I . . .

I opened my bedroom window yesterday and standing in the middle of my yard was a . . .

One night after I fed my cat, he started to grow and *grow* and GROW. The next thing I knew, . . .

I was swimming under the water. All of a sudden it got very dark. I looked behind me and saw a. . . . Then I . . .

I bought a magic lollipop at the magic shop. I took one taste and . . .

I went camping with my friends. We put up our tents and when I was sound asleep I felt something in my sleeping bag with me. It was a . . .

On my way home from school yesterday, I found a baby dinosaur under a bush. I took it home and . . .

I am a big black spider. Name four reasons why you do or don't like me.

Write a story using these four words: cactus, marshmallow, horse, bike.

Pretend you are going to build a play fort using only food items. Write what you would build it with and draw a picture of what it would look like.

How would you spend $100? Make a list. $1,000?

Make up new colors for snow, rain, mud, grass, clouds, sky, people. Draw a picture of how your new world would look.

Write a letter to the president, Mother Nature, the Cat in the Hat, the principal, your pet, any storybook character, your favorite author.

The Art Center

The art table is a center that remains at the back of my room throughout the year. An old dropleaf kitchen table is ideal. Kept at the back of this table are a wide variety of primary art resource books. In the rare event that a child elects to use this center without a preconceived project, he or she will find hundreds of ideas to choose from. Children especially like to try cartooning. Most children's book clubs offer cartooning "how to" paperbacks as bonus selections to the teacher who orders from them. It doesn't take long to build a wide selection for your class. The children's sections of most book and toy stores also offer many kinds of art project books in paperback.

On this table, place many sizes, colors, and textures of papers, including origami, tissue, crepe, and construction. Include a variety of scrap materials, such as cardboard, poster board, foam board, felt, fabric, string, and yarn. Pipe cleaners, cotton balls, glitter, sponge chunks, drinking straws, Styrofoam packing shapes, egg cartons, foam meat trays, and other treasure trash can be there too. Send a list of trash items you would like for your classroom home to parents and you will soon have more than you need. In a box under the table are watercolors, poster paints, crayons, markers, scissors, rulers, and colored pencils.

This center is quite large and allows room for three or four students to create at one time. Children may take materials to their desks as well. Each child is responsible for leaving the center as organized and clean as he or she found it. This takes a little extra monitoring initially! Be sure you have large sponges at your sink for spills and cleanup. Save old blouses and shirts for children to use as "sloppy smocks." You will soon find that almost every learning activity, from social studies to spelling, can lead to a wonderful art-related experience. Encourage your children to discover these creative links on their own. If the materials aren't readily available at all times, your students may miss far too many opportunities to enrich and cement new concepts.

Jigsaw Puzzle Center

If you have a little extra space somewhere in your room, a jigsaw puzzle center will be put to good use on indoor recess days or whenever you have children who simply have run out of things to do. Keep a rather complicated one available at all times and let everyone enjoy adding a few pieces during the day. A good source for used puzzles is the salvage store. A note to parents will supply you with many more. Children can create their own puzzles by pasting a large magazine picture onto a piece of tag or cardboard and then cutting it into interesting shapes. Keep the pieces in a manila envelope when not in use.

Memory Center

When a couple of children have a few minutes of free time, let them go to a quiet corner and play a memory game or two. Provide a box filled with small objects and a few egg cartons. (Ask your students to provide things for this box from their discarded toys.) One child selects a few things and places them in the sections of the egg carton. The other child studies them for a minute and then the lid is closed. The object of the game is to see how many things the observer can remember. Even trickier is to try to remember the exact order of the articles in the carton. Then the children trade roles. Older children can write down all the objects they can remember.

I often do this activity in small groups as well. It is fun to choose a child as leader and join the game yourself. It's harder than you think!

Symmetry Center

Gather large magazine pictures of faces, animals, or other subjects that can be cut in half symmetrically. Mount one half on tagboard and have children choose one that interests them. Lay the half-object on a sheet of plain paper and instruct the children to complete the other half of the picture. This is an activity you may need to model for young children.

Use these half-finished drawings for another symmetry activity. Ask the children to complete the other half of each picture and then add as many details as it takes to make the drawing into a recognizable object. Have a sharing session so each child gets to talk about a few of his or her creations. Send enough copies of this next activity home for an entire family and ask that they complete the pictures as their fancy dictates (fig. 6.1, p. 106). Be sure the child gets to share the family's efforts when he or she brings them back.

Alphabet Center

Create several different kinds of alphabet sets for your students to use to practice spelling words and alphabetical order activities. Several children can work at this center at one time. Fill a canning jar or basket with lima beans on which you have written all the letters (one on each side of the bean). Be sure to make extra vowels. Then your students can play a game I call "Spill the Beans." Choose a child to be the caller for the group. He or she calls out one of this week's spelling words; then the children Spill the Beans and try to be the first one to assemble the letters in the correct order. The winner becomes the next word caller. Or the children can create the alphabet as quickly as possible. Perhaps they would like to create all of the names of the children in their group. For kindergartners or first-graders, you can pronounce a word and have them find the beginning or ending sound.

A volunteer or parent with sewing skills can whip up a cloth bag with a drawstring and fill it with a complete set of letters for each child in your class to keep at his or her desk. When there are a few extra moments, you can have every child participate in word activities right in their own seats.

The small alphabet noodles sold in the pasta section of the grocery store can be used in much the same way. I sometimes cook up a batch of these and ladle them onto a plastic dessert plate for each child; then we play a word game I call "Eat Your Words." Again, I call out a spelling word or the name of a student. When everyone has arranged the noodles in the proper order, we eat them!

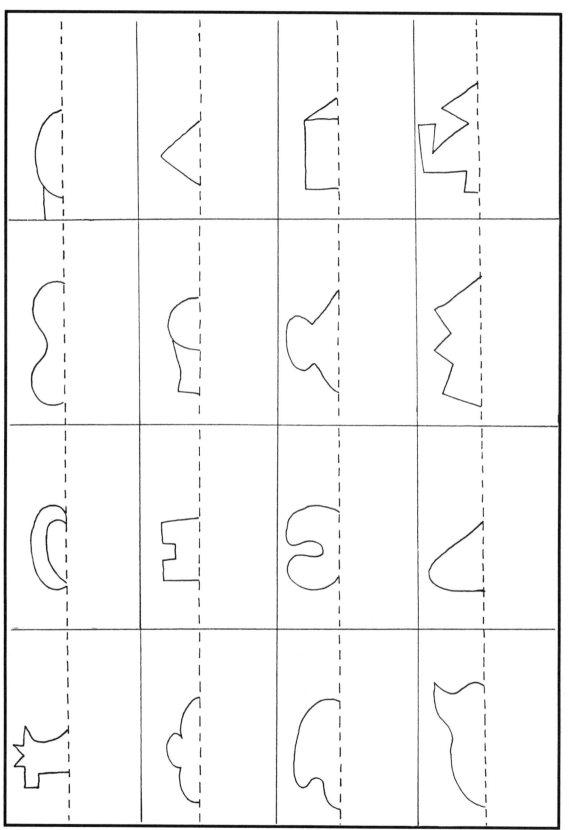

Fig. 6.1. Symmetry figures.

The letter tiles from discarded Scrabble and other letter games are also an inexpensive way to build an alphabet collection to use in the alphabet center. Don't forget to get some magnetic letters so your students can make words on the end of your desk or on the sides of the filing cabinet. Magnetic letters can be stored on an old cookie sheet for convenience.

◆ Food Labels and Containers

At the alphabet center, I also keep several empty food containers, such as cereal boxes, instant dinner boxes, pasta bags, and labels from soup, vegetables, and other canned goods. My first-graders are given the task of tallying how many A's, B's, C's, and so on, they can find on one container or label. Older children learn to read the contents, weight, ingredients, and recipes found there. Or I can have them arrange the containers by size, alphabetical order, weight, food group, and so on. Sometimes I tape prices to these items and have the children add up a grocery list.

Magazine Search Centers

Collect dozens of discarded supermarket, homemaker's, and other appropriate magazines and you'll never run out of interesting projects for children in all grades. Make little blank booklets for these centers by cutting photocopy paper in half and stapling the sides together, about ten pages per book. The children cut up the magazines as they find the pictures they need. Some of the projects you can assign are:

1. The Four Food Groups; or Green Foods, Red Foods, Brown Foods, etc.

2. Healthy Foods and Junk Foods

3. Transportation

4. Jobs and Careers

5. Buildings and Homes

6. Hobbies and Sports

7. Animals

8. Flowers and Plants

9. My Word Book

10. A Book of Colors

11. Big Things, Little Things

12. My Number Book (1 bike, 2 oranges, 3 dogs, etc.)

13. Things I Can Hear

14. Things I Wear

15. My Book of Feelings

These category books can be an ongoing activity throughout the year. Write in the names of objects for small children. They will delight in being able to read them later on.

Centers to Go

Collect pictures from old greeting cards, magazines, and story books. Trim and mount on tagboard. Place three to five pictures, some lined writing paper, and a pencil in nine-by-six manila envelopes from the school office, or sandwich bags that seal, for a take-home writing packet. Enclose a note that says;

> Dear Parent,
>
> _____ would like to write a story about one of the pictures in this envelope. Please encourage your child by providing a quiet place and a little time to work uninterrupted. You may help as needed. Please return the envelope when your child feels the project is completed. Thank you for sharing this writing activity with us.
>
> | YOUR PERSONAL STAMP | Miss Jones

You can also mount an intriguing picture on tagboard, cut it up jigsaw-style, and place it in an envelope for a similar take-home writing project.

Other packets for home study can be made by cutting up and laminating articles from old *Ranger Rick*, *Owl*, *National Geographic for Children*, and other science-based magazines for children. On the envelope, print the topic of interest enclosed, and write a few questions to be answered by the child when he or she has finished the reading. I find this application for children's magazines very appropriate, as students will make much better use of the information when it is broken down into smaller topics.

Other home study packets that are portable, when filled with a few pieces of graph paper, colored pencils, and intriguing ideas:

1. Design your IDEAL bedroom

2. Design the IDEAL playground

3. Design the IDEAL classroom

4. Design the IDEAL school

5. Design the IDEAL backyard

6.   Design the IDEAL playroom

7.   Design the IDEAL school desk

8.   Design an IDEAL planet

9.   Design the IDEAL pet

10.   Design the IDEAL zoo

◆ Getting Centers Back and Forth in One Piece

Old plastic lunch boxes from the lost-and-found box or salvage store make very handy and easy-to-tote containers for projects that go home. Canvas bags with cloth handles can be found in most hobby supply stores. I have had an artistic mom stencil these bags with colorful pictures. I made a one-time investment of enough bags for each child in my class, put a number inside, and encouraged the children to check these bags out to carry home library books, home assignments, and reports. We have only lost one bag and that was in a tragic house fire.

Chalkboard Centers

Find a few 9-x-12-inch writing slates. Provide chalk and several assignments on 9-x-12-inch tagboard, on which you have modeled a cursive or manuscript writing task. Number the lessons and provide a numbered checkoff sheet for each child so that they may check their writing with you before erasing and going on. These chalkboards can also be used for extra spelling or math facts practice and geometry tasks.

Teacher supply stores have soft plastic pencil grips designed for primary pencils, but they also make excellent chalk holders. Many children dislike the feel of holding a piece of chalk. An old receiving blanket or old flannel shirt torn in small pieces makes great slate erasers. The new dry-erase boards in slate size are wonderful and inexpensive for these same activities. I found mine at a teacher supply store, but I notice that hardware and discount stores are now carrying them, too.

The Overhead Projector

An overhead projector has become one of my most valuable tools. Equipped with a colorful set of overhead markers, several sheets of various colors of acetate overlays, and a variety of miniatures and cut-outs of animals and objects, I can teach just about any concept I want, incorporating and complementing any and all centers and activities. Turning off all the classroom lights gets everybody focused and attentive on the lesson at hand.

Activities for Kindergarten

For kindergartners, I use the overhead projector to teach handwriting by modeling the correct formation of each letter and number. The children can also write on the overhead, and love to see their first efforts "in lights." Counting and numbers are so much easier to teach when corresponding miniature manipulatives are projected in shadow on the screen. The confetti shapes, such as cats, pumpkins, animals, apples, rabbits, and so on, sold in greeting card stores are ideal for projection. You can also use plastic chips or beans for counting. I keep the focus of the lesson at a low height so that a child can take a pointing stick, go to the screen, and become the presenter. Children also enjoy writing their numbers on the projector and putting up the appropriate number of objects to show their classmates their skills. Letters are fun to teach by writing on the screen or projecting felt cut-outs or alphabet noodles. Cut out the main characters of a fairy tale or favorite story and have the children sequence them on the overhead.

◆ **Teaching Colors on the Overhead**

When teaching a lesson on color recognition and blending, put some water in a clear glass dish on the overhead and drop red, yellow, and blue food coloring into the water. Listen for the oooh's and ahhh's as the dyes run together, forming secondary colors. You can also achieve a similar effect by overlapping circles of colored acetate on the screen. Follow up this lesson with the children's first watercolor paintings.

Activities for First Grade

First-graders learn sound blending more quickly when I cut out colored acetate train cars, one letter written in the center of each, and place them on the screen of the overhead projector. I teach the sounds the letters make for the first few weeks and then begin the decoding skill of sound blending by making the little train cars bump into each other. I also teach word families in this manner. The children always like to participate in creating new words and coming to the overhead to be the teacher. When they first begin to read whole phrases, get out the overhead and write some CLOZE sentences. Write the words to be chosen from on little colored acetate slips so that the children can come up and manipulate the words to complete the sentences.

Activities for Second Grade

Second-graders can be taught to tell the time on the overhead projector if you make an acetate clock face and hands. They can also practice counting acetate replicas of money. Try presenting new sight vocabulary lessons from your reading teacher's guide on the overhead instead of the usual charts. Almost any worksheet can be better introduced in this way. Ask your school secretary for a little in-service training on how to make overheads from your worksheets or literature selections.

Activities for Third Grade

Third-graders thrive on speed-reading contests. Make an acetate overhead reproduction of a highly motivating passage of your reading lessons. Send home copies for the children to practice with their parents. Then get out a stopwatch and hold a speed-reading contest. Choose a scorekeeper, a timer, and the first reader. Put the selection on the overhead and sit back to watch the fun. Offer different selections for each level of reading ability so that everyone has a chance to win now and then. When I first began this activity with my Chapter I readers, I thought the competition might stifle my slowest readers. On the contrary, my slowest reader now wins these contests as often as anyone else.

Compound words are a breeze to teach if you put them on colored strips, cut apart the two words, and have the children work in teams by putting a line down the middle of the screen and letting them see how quickly they can match up two words that make sense. Reproduce a fairly difficult crossword puzzle and leave it projected on a large sheet of paper taped to a wall, off and on all day. When children have finished their other work, they may go to the puzzle and add a word or two.

Art in the Dark

Sometime this year, have an "Art in the Dark" show. Provide a blank sheet of acetate to every child and have them each create a beautiful piece of art using markers. This would make a good center activity. If your school doesn't have cardboard acetate borders, create your own frames with tagboard. When everyone has a completed masterpiece, have an art appreciation afternoon. Turn out the lights, set up the overhead projector, and have each child present his or her art to the class, explaining the picture and how he or she did it. The pictures can then be permanently mounted on white paper or hung just as they are in a window.

Replacing Overhead Bulbs

If you must replace a burned-out light bulb, ask for help the first time. If you touch a light bulb with your fingers, the oil from your skin will cause the light bulb to burn out again very quickly, and these bulbs are *very* expensive. Let the projector cool off for a few minutes each hour to prevent it from overheating.

There is probably not one unit of study that cannot be supplemented by activities involving the overhead projector. I would be hard pressed to try to demonstrate art activities, science, nutrition, social studies, math, or handwriting without it. Once you have put a few little objects on the screen, you will probably be hooked. Put one in your room and experiment with the possibilities as soon as possible.

Conclusion

Centers are the lifeblood of my classroom. They provide my students with independence, challenges, experiences, and variety. Listen to your children and pick up on their interests. We often forget that there are so many little things children don't know: What does it mean to line up? Where does bacon come from? What's in Jello? Why are old teachers wrinkled? Centers can be anything from apples to zippers. The learning that goes on at them and the time spent putting them together may be the best thing I do for my students. The following resources will help you with hundreds of ideas—if you have time after the children have given you theirs.

Resources

(Note: The asterisk [*] denotes titles I believe are most helpful to first year teachers.)

Abbott, Janet. *Learn to Fold—Fold to Learn.* Franklin Mathematics Series. Chicago: Lyons & Carnahan, 1970.

Allison, Linda, and David Katz. *Gee, Wiz!* Covela, Calif.: Yolla Bolly Press, 1982.

Bird, Lois Bridges, ed. *Becoming a Whole Language School.* Katonah, N.Y.: Richard C. Owens, 1989.

Black, Irma Simonton. *Busy Seeds.* New York: Holiday House, 1970.

Bohning, Gerry, Ann Phillips, and Sandra H. Bryant. *Literature on the Move—Making and Using Pop-Up and Lift-Flap Books.* Englewood, Colo.: Teacher Ideas Press, 1993.

Comins, Jeremy. *Art from Found Objects.* New York: Lothrop, Lee & Shepard, 1974.

Corwin, Judith. *Messner Holiday Library.* New York: Simon & Schuster, 1983.

The Creative Curriculum for Early Childhood. 3d ed. Washington, D.C.: Teaching Strategies, 1992.

DeBruin, Jerry. *Creative, Hands-On Science Experiences Using Free and Inexpensive Materials.* Carthage, Ill.: Good Apple, 1986.

Forte, Imogene, Mary Ann Pangle, and Robbie Tupa. *Center Stuff for Nooks, Crannies and Corners.* Nashville, Tenn.: Incentive Publications, 1973.

———. *Crayons and Markers.* Nashville, Tenn.: Incentive Publications, 1987.

———. *The Tabletop Learning Series.* Nashville, Tenn.: Incentive Publications, 1987.

Frank, Marjorie. *Complete Writing Lessons for the Primary Grades.* Nashville, Tenn.: Incentive Publications, 1987.

Hass, Carolyn Buhai. *The Big Book of Recipes for Fun.* Glencoe, Ill.: CBH, 1980.

Heilman, Arthur W., and Elizabeth Ann Holmes. *Smuggling Language into the Teaching of Reading.* Columbus, Ohio: Charles E. Merrill, 1972.

Jenkins, L., and P. McLean. *It's a Tangram World.* San Leandro, Calif.: Educational Science Consultants, 1971.

*Jensen, Janice. *Literature-Based Learning Activities Kit.* West Nyack, N.Y.: Center for Applied Research in Education, 1991.

Jones, H., and D. Horlock. *Fun with Geometric Activities.* Englewood Cliffs, N.J.: Prentice-Hall Learning Systems, 1974.

*Kaplan, Sandra Nina, JoAnn Butom Kaplan, Sheila Kunishima Madsen, and Bette K. Taylor. *Change for Children—Ideas and Activities for Individualizing Learning.* Pacific Palisades, Calif.: Goodyear, 1973.

Katzer, Sonia, and Christine A. Crnkovich. *From Scribblers to Scribes: Young Writers Use the Computer*. Englewood, Colo.: Teacher Ideas Press, 1991.

Mandry, Kathy, and Joe Toto. *How to Grow a Jelly Glass Farm*. New York: Random House, 1974.

McVitty, Walter. *Getting It Together—Reading Writing Classroom*. Rozelle, Australia: Primary English Teaching Association, 1986.

Olsen, Mary Lou. *Creative Connections: Literature and the Reading Program, Grades 1-3*. Littleton, Colo.: Libraries Unlimited, 1987.

Pigdon, Keith, and Marilyn Woolley. *Earthworms*. Cleveland, Ohio: Modern Curriculum Press, 1989.

*Poppe, Carol A., and Nancy A. VanMatre. *Science Learning Centers for the Primary Grades*. West Nyack, N.Y.: Center for Applied Research in Education, 1985.

Rights, Mollie. *Beastly Neighbors*. Boston: Little, Brown, 1981.

*Rybak, Sharon. *Launching a Great Year*. Carthage, Ill.: Good Apple, 1989.

Seymour, Dale, and Joyce Snider. *Line Designs*. Palo Alto, Calif.: Creative Publications, 1968.

Shape and Size: The Nuffield Mathematics Project. New York: John Wiley & Sons, 1969.

Smith, E. Brooks, and Kenneth S. Goodman. *Language and Thinking in the Elementary School*. New York: Holt, Rinehart & Winston, 1970.

Smith, James A. *Creative Teaching of Reading in the Elementary School*. 2d ed. Boston: Allyn & Bacon, 1975.

Snoddon, Ruth V. *Library Skills Activities for the Primary Grades*. West Nyack, N.Y.: Center for Applied Research in Education, 1987.

Stein, Sara. *The Science Book*. New York: Workman, 1979.

Walter, Marion. *Boxes, Squares, and Other Things*. Washington, D.C.: National Council of Teachers of Mathematics, 1970.

7
Seasonal Activities

Holidays, such as Halloween, Thanksgiving, Chanukah, Christmas, Valentine's Day, and many others, are often used as foci for classroom units of study, art activities, and parties. Because all of these special days have underlying religious significance, you may sooner or later have a family, community group, or administration that raises objections to the use of instructional time for teaching holiday-related materials.

In this chapter you will find many ideas for seasonal, rather than holiday, related teaching activities. You will learn how to create whole learning experiences using a thematic approach. Most of these units were developed cooperatively with families that requested I not include their children in any holiday activities during class time. I have also supplied a monthly calendar of special days and weeks that suggests interesting topics of study for future planning.

Thematic Units

I began eliminating all holiday activities from my personal curriculum many years ago. I have enjoyed the challenges and variety of planning experiences in which *all* my students may participate.

Because there are so many excellent books, kits, and other resources available at teacher supply stores, bookstores, and in teachers' manuals, here I outline just a few seasonal ideas and suggest where you may look further for more. The pumpkin unit is one I developed several years ago. It is a fully expanded topic of study incorporating every curricular area. This type of cross-curricular planning can be used with all of the topics I suggest. Once you have built one unit, you will know the simple techniques for building a unit on any topic imaginable. I begin planning units with an outline similar to the one shown in figure 7.1, page 116, and then let my resources and students' interests lead the way.

A PATTERN FOR DEVELOPING
A WHOLE LANGUAGE UNIT ON RABBITS

MOTIVATIONAL ACTIVITIES

RESOURCES

BOOKS AND MAGAZINES

READING ACTIVITIES

LANGUAGE ACTIVITIES

SCIENCE AND SOCIAL STUDIES

ART ACTIVITIES

HANDS ON ACTIVITIES

MUSIC DRAMA MOVEMENT

OTHER

Fig. 7.1. Unit outline pattern.

Fall Activities

Pumpkins

During September and October, portly, ripe pumpkins abound at nearly every supermarket and roadside stand. They play a major role in the celebration of Halloween, but they offer a much richer source of study than you may have imagined. Consider using several pumpkins in your primary classroom in some of these non-Halloween ways. (Some of the other gourds and squashes of the fall season lend themselves to these activities as well.)

◆ Science and Math

Provide a nice, fat pumpkin for each group of four or five children. Guide them to investigate their pumpkins in some of these ways:

1. Observe, feel, and write down the number of creases on the outside of your pumpkin. Is there an even or odd number of lines? Do the lines run all the way from the stem to the bottom? Close your eyes and figure out a way to count the creases again without peeking. Are all pumpkins the exact same color? Put your pumpkin on a scale and see how much it weighs. Weigh it again after you take out all the insides.

2. Smell the outside of the pumpkin. Cut a lid in the pumpkin. Smell the inside of the pumpkin. Who likes the smell? Who doesn't? Why?

3. Lift the lid off very carefully, pulling with it as much of the inside as possible. Does each seed have its own string? What is the string for? Are the seeds pointy side up or down? How do they feel? What shape are they?

4. Do bigger pumpkins have bigger seeds? Do bigger pumpkins have more seeds than smaller ones? Was your pumpkin mostly full of seeds or mostly empty? Estimate how many seeds you think are in your pumpkin.

5. Remove all the seeds and strings. Throw away all of the strings. Put the seeds in rows of ten and then count all the seeds. How close was your estimation of the number of seeds? Compare the number of seeds in your pumpkin to the number of seeds in another group's pumpkin.

6. Look inside your pumpkin. Did the creases come all the way through? Use a ruler to measure the thickness of your pumpkin. Which group has the fattest pumpkin?

7. Fill the sink with water. Put your pumpkin in the water. Does it float or sink? Put some seeds in the water. Do they float or sink? Put the lid in the water. Does it float or sink?

8. Think of some things you can do with your pumpkin. Could you use it for a vase for flowers? Could you eat it? What animals might eat a pumpkin?

There is an unusual little white decorative gourd in the stores each fall that dries out very nicely if the outer skin is not pierced. (The skin has an almost brain-like appearance.) I have several dried ones on my science table and I enjoy watching and listening to my new students try to figure out what they are. I keep a "GUESS" jar on the table and encourage children to write their guesses on slips of paper, to be tallied and discussed later in the year. Most of the guesses are the brain of some small animal.

◆ Reading and Research

Take the children to the school library and search for books about pumpkins. This is a good opportunity to begin the use of a primary set of encyclopedias. The librarian or media specialist should be able to help you find an array of materials.

Set up a classroom library and use it as a center to research the squash family. Divide the class into groups to find the answers to these questions:

1. In what food group do pumpkins belong?

2. Are they a vegetable or a fruit?

3. How much can a pumpkin weigh?

4. What vitamins are in a pumpkin?

5. Is there a male pumpkin plant and a female pumpkin plant? How are they different?

6. What does a pumpkin plant look like?

7. Where did pumpkins originate?

8. How long have pumpkins been on the earth?

9. What plant family do pumpkins belong to?

Note: Some of these investigations lead naturally into a segment on nutrition (see later in this unit).

◆ Spelling

Select a few pumpkin-related words to add to your weekly spelling list, such as *seeds, pulp, skin, stem, vine,* or *plant.* For second- and third-graders, give each child a paper with the words F-A-L-L P-U-M-P-K-I-N-S at the top and see how many words they can generate using only these letters (e.g., *skin, in, mall, pup, lap,* etc.).

◆**Poetry**

Even the greatest poets found the beautiful pumpkin an irresistible subject for writing. I use the following Sandburg poem to help students begin to see the pumpkin in its natural setting and to tie together writing and art activities. After discussing the poet's words and meanings, let children generate landscape art using construction and tissue paper. Have children choose tissue papers the color of the sky, morning, full daylight, or evening. Then choose colors for autumn hills and fields. Using watered-down school glue, cover an entire sheet of white construction paper with this mixture. Tear tissue paper into pieces to cover the construction paper to suggest the background and rebrush over the top with the glue mixture again. Allow the background to dry for a couple of hours or overnight. Then add construction paper details such as trees, bushes, barns in the distance, cornstalks, and the pumpkins. The results are breathtaking.

Theme in Yellow

I spot the hills
With yellow balls in autumn
I light the prairie cornfields
Orange and tawny gold clusters
And I am called pumpkins.

—Carl Sandburg

Brainstorm as many ideas as possible about pumpkins with the children. Web their ideas on a large sheet of orange bulletin-board paper, cut in the shape of a giant pumpkin, and taped to the chalkboard. Display this web somewhere in the room for several days so that children have access to this vocabulary for writing activities that may include original stories, artwork, songs, riddles, poetry, or recipes.

Help each child do an acrostic or haiku poem on a pumpkin-shaped paper—orange, of course. It may be impossible to keep the jack-o-lantern idea out of all your discussions, but you *are* offering many options and ideas for children who cannot participate in Halloween activities.

The following is one of the most creative *acrostic* poems I have ever seen, written by a second-grader (unedited). This type of poem is created by putting all of the letters of the subject in a vertical column and then using the letters as the first letters for words that describe the subject of the poem.

P — purkee
U — uglee
M— munstrly
P — pi bownd
K — kitchin brownd
I — impee
N — nit liter

—Peter H., grade 2

The next example is a *haiku* poem. This poetry format is characterized by three lines, the first line having five syllables; the second, seven syllables; and the third, five syllables.

> Pumpkin sitting there
> You drank the sun all summer
> Now I eat you up
>
> —Adam K., grade 2

The *diamante* poem form consists of seven lines. The final poem has a diamond shape when completed.

Line 1: noun (subject of poem)	Pumpkin
Line 2: two adjectives	Golden, chubby
Line 3: three verbs or "ing" words	Plumping, growing, rolling
Line 4: four-word phrase	Always beautiful to me
Line 5: three verbs or "ing" words	Sunning, vining, seeding
Line 6: two more adjectives	Lined, stemmy
Line 7: a synonym for the main subject	Gourd

> Emmy H., grade 2

Another poetry form is the *simple couplet*, two lines of verse that rhyme. The rap music craze has had one positive impact on my young students: they know how to rhyme!

> Pumpkin! Pumpkin! On my wall.
> I see you 'most every fall.
>
> Teneika W., grade 2

◆ Art

Poems are not, of course, the only things that can motivate your students' artistic endeavors. Have children bring in a variety of fruits from the squash and gourd family for the centerpiece of a fall display. The turban squash is one of my favorites and has been the motivation for many a creative writing piece. Inspired by this fall still life of pumpkins, Indian corn, gourds, leaves, shocks of straw, corn, wheat, and so on, there are many art activities your class can undertake. Set out the temperas, water colors, crayons, markers, construction paper, tissue paper, and let the ideas roll.

Create a fall pendant or necklace of pumpkins and apples made of fun dough. This is my recipe for a pliable and lasting mixture, which it can be used for many different activities. Your children will taste it only once.

1 cup flour
½ cup salt
1 cup water
2 teaspoons cream of tartar
1 tablespoon vegetable oil
a few drops food coloring

Mix all ingredients in a saucepan. Keep stirring and heat slowly. The mixture will thicken immediately. Dump it out on a piece of waxed paper or plastic wrap, knead for a minute, and wrap tightly. It feels wonderful! For scented play dough, add to this recipe a few drops of food flavoring, such as almond, vanilla, peppermint, cinnamon, or wintergreen.

Show children how to make small pumpkins, apples, and leaves from the dough. Poke a hole through each piece with a large tapestry needle, lunchroom straw, or skewer, and allow to air dry for three to five days. Arrange on a sturdy yarn or string. These necklaces can also be used as counting beads for kindergartners and first-graders.

Another harvesttime necklace that is interesting, and edible, is made by having children bring in apples, carrots, parsnips, oranges, raisins, prunes, figs, frozen peas, celery, peaches, or apricots. Enlist a parent volunteer to help each child slice these foods very thin and, with a tapestry needle and yarn, string them for drying. In about a week, the children will have a fruit and vegetable jerky much like the ones that Native Americans and the pioneers made to help them survive the winters of long ago. You can hurry the process by putting the necklaces on a cookie sheet in an oven set at 100 degrees overnight.

The fall harvest season is a good time to try seed mosaics. Cover the art table with a wide variety of seeds, including corn, many sizes and colors of beans, sunflower seeds, dried pumpkin seeds, and brown and white rice. Let children glue the seeds to a piece of tagboard on which they have drawn a design or fall picture. The colors are subtle and the textures lovely.

◆ Nutrition

Have children brainstorm some recipes for pumpkin pie or cookies. Allow them to contribute all ideas without censure. The ingredients, amounts, and methods of preparation will surprise you. Conceal your amusement as best you can and write all ideas on the board or chart paper to be kept for a class cookbook. This book can be compiled throughout the year as you celebrate other seasons and then given as a heartwarming gift for Mothers' Day in May or a cookbook for Thanksgiving.

Ask the children to bring in pumpkin pie or cookie recipes from home. Choose one, reproduce it for each student to read, and let the children prepare their own pumpkin treats at school. Compare their recipes with tried-and-true ones. Or, if you're very brave, use one of the children's recipes as an experiment.

You might even use one of the class pumpkins for the main ingredient. Most children never associate canned pumpkin with the real thing. Clean one, cut it into chunks, add some water, and let it simmer in a large pot on a hot plate in the back of the room.

Of course, you can toast all the seeds from the class pumpkins by spraying them with a nonstick shortening spray, sprinkling them with seasoned salt, and baking them at 300 degrees for 30 minutes.

These are just a few of the activities inspired by the fruits of the harvest season. It is always my favorite time of the year. I hope you'll try a few of them to get your feet wet, and then invent your own as you venture away from the teacher's guides. After reading through the pumpkin unit, I think you will see how one small topic can be expanded to include almost every curriculum area. The remainder of this chapter gives you further suggestions. Its Resources section will give you other resources for cross-curricular ideas.

Skeletons and Bones

Skeletons and bones are other topics that are very much on the minds of children around Halloween time. Instead of dwelling on the spooky nature of these objects, take advantage of children's curiosity and embark on an anatomy unit. Send a letter to parents outlining your unit and ask if they have any animal bones to contribute. Here in Colorado, many students in my classes have a hunter or two in their families and are always able to loan us a few specimens. Your district's high school biology department would probably also share some of its bone collection with you for a few days.

There are several fine primary-level films that you can check out from your district media center to get your unit off to a good start. Acquire a good collection of primary-level science books, magazines, and other printed materials for your students to use throughout this unit. Ask your media center technician to help you.

Hang a life-size blow-up skeleton in the classroom, or make tagboard skeletons that are authentically jointed and assembled with brads. Label the major bones. These words can become your spelling list for second-, third-, and fourth-graders.

Get a few owl pellets through your science supervisor and dissect one on the overhead. Show the children how to reassemble a mouse skeleton from the findings in the owl pellet; then divide the class into study groups of three or four children and let each group dissect its own owl pellet. Compare the femurs of mice to those of other animals and human beings to note the similarities and differences.

Provide a few X-rays for the children to examine. Put them on the overhead projector for a closer look. Your physician will probably give you old X-rays when he or she learns what you are doing with them.

Have children save chicken, pork, and beef bones from their school lunches and home meals. These bones can be cleaned and dried as described in chapter 6. Keep these bones in a center so the children can create the skeletons of an imaginary animal. After gluing the bones on cardboard, the students can draw an outline around them to show how their creatures would look. They can finish the project by writing a story about a day in the life of their animals.

Discuss the importance of proper nutrition to the development of the skeletal system. Your district will undoubtedly have a few primary films in its collection about the human skeletal structure, as well as nutrition basics.

Native American Contributions

Prior to Thanksgiving, have a mini-unit on the foods we eat that were first introduced to the European settlers by the Native Americans. It is said that the Pilgrims would have perished had it not been for Massasoit, the Algonquin chief, who taught them how to grow and store corn. The Indians also showed them the value of the native squashes, beans, pumpkins, apples, and sweet potatoes. They introduced the early settlers to a variety of edible berries, roots, nuts, herbs, onions (*Chicago* means "stinking onion"), and bulbs. The Ojibway Indians of the Northeast discovered the process of making syrup and candy from the sap of the sugar-maple tree. You could celebrate the foods given to us by the Native Americans by serving up some candied sweet potatoes, popcorn, and sunflower seeds. The children could also create a bulletin board bursting with the bounty of the season.

Other Topics for Fall Activities

1. Animals that will soon begin hibernation.

2. Native American pottery.

3. Fall leaves (collect and dry them, then laminate and cut into bookmarks).

4. Spiders (a popular Halloween creature).

5. The Three Little Pigs (building shelters for winter).

6. Cats (a Halloween-related animal).

7. Apples.

8. Fall trees (rendered with a variety of art media).

Winter Activities

Snowmen

Constructing paper snowmen is a perennial favorite for primary students, so don't miss the opportunities this topic holds for science, math, reading, and art. Many art activities are enhanced by using the colorful paper from discarded wallpaper books. Call a nearby wallpaper dealer and ask when you can pick up some of the outdated sample books. These dealers are more than happy to give them to you rather than put them in the dumpster. Children can cut the three paper circles for the snowman's head and body freehand, or you can make patterns from tagboard for them to trace. Make patterns for mittens, hats, and scarves so that the children can trace these and cut them from wallpaper patterns of their choice. Eyes and mouths can be little black paper circles. The nose can be an elongated triangle made from orange construction paper. Arms can be paper twigs, or you and the children can don coats and hats and go for a neighborhood walk to gather the real things. A row of decked-out snowmen holding mittened hands on the wall in the hallway is a whimsical sight in the dead of winter.

Hundredth Day

Sometime in January (you'll have to count the actual school days attended in your own district's calendar), you might like to celebrate the Hundredth Day of school. Primary-age children have very little understanding of this huge number, and this is one concrete way to help them visualize its enormity. You might begin this activity by having a child put up the number one on the first day of school on a special chart or post the numbers on slips of paper along the baseboard of the classroom. Each school day, continue the numberline, and on the Hundredth Day have a special celebration.

Students might spend the day working in teams composing a variety of posters containing 100 objects. Posters might display 100 pieces of pasta shapes, pennies, thumbtacks, paper clips, beans, or any other readily available, small objects. Other collage-type posters can be composed by cutting out magazine pictures: 100 toys, 100 babies, 100 vegetables, 100 cars, 100 desserts, or 100 anything you can think of. One year I assigned a letter of the alphabet to each team and they had to find 100 letter M's or P's, or another letter in magazines to complete their posters. At the end of the day we celebrated by eating 100 pieces of popcorn each, swished down with fruit punch.

Other Topics for Winter Activities

1. Make fortune cookies and put loving messages inside. Recipe in Suzanne Barchers's *Creating and Managing the Literate Classroom* (see Resources for chapter 3).

2. Make hearts-and-flowers love necklaces from construction paper cutouts.

3. Study mask making around the world and make a few types.

4. Build a cardboard city using paper boxes of all sizes, and paper cylinders from toilet tissue, paper towels, and gift wrap tubes. Create a street plan for the layout. Don't forget to invent a park to play in!

5. Do an ocean unit and set up an aquarium.

6. Have each child bring in pennies dated for each year of his or her life. Create a chart and write something memorable from each year next to the appropriate penny.

7. Build a log cabin from cardboard carpet rolls or paper towel rolls.

8. Paint a winter scene using only white paper and black tempera paint.

9. Work in pairs to trace around each other's hands to create unique "mittens" or "gloves" for a bulletin board border.

10. Have everyone bring in their favorite thing to sleep with and sit around and tell stories all afternoon.

11. End an expanded nutrition unit with a grand-scale tasting party or luncheon. Get some parents involved in this one.

Spring Activities

Little Red Riding Hood

Early spring seems to be the ideal time for one of my favorite activities: corresponding with a beloved storybook character. A few days after we have read and compared several versions of *Little Red Riding Hood*, the class receives a handwritten letter from Little Red herself! The text of her letter goes something like this, although it varies depending on any social issues currently of pertinence to my students:

Dear Third Graders at Washington School,

I need your help! As you know, I recently had a very close call with a vicious wolf. I still shake all over when I think about it!

First of all, my mother and father are divorced. I have to live with my mother in the deep, dark woods. I would really like to spend more time with my dad, but he lives in the city. What can I do?

Next, my mother sends me on errands every day through the dark and dangerous woods to my grandmother's cottage. My grandmother is eighty years old and can't do very much to take care of herself anymore. Poor old dear! I love her a lot but I am scared to go in the woods alone anymore after what happened last week with that wolf. What can I do?

Another thing: I have no one to play with and I get really bored. If you were me, how would you have fun living way out here in the woods? We don't even have a TV.

And one last thing, I hate this red riding hood my mother makes me wear all the time. What do the girls wear at your school? Could you draw me some pictures of really neat girl's outfits? Maybe my mother could make some new clothes for me.

Please write back to me and give me some ideas to help me with my problems. I promise to write back and tell you how I am doing.

Your Friend,

Red

P.S. I want to change my name! Any ideas? Thanks for your help!

As with the Joseph story in chapter 4, there will be a few raised eyebrows, but everyone wants to "play the game," so we discuss the letter thoroughly. Then the class learns the proper way to format a letter and envelope so that each child can write an own personal response to Little Red. With first- and second-graders, a class letter, jointly written, is more appropriate.

Some of the replies I have seen over the years are quite poignant and revealing. Many of my students can really identify with the single-parent status of this little girl and others have clever ideas for relocating Grandmother and outfoxing the wolf. Some of the girls go through catalogs to find clothing ideas to send along in their letters.

After the letters have been proofed and rewritten, the children use rubber stamps or stickers to substitute for the stamp required in the upper right-hand corner of the envelope. Meanwhile, we learn about the cancellation of stamps, return addressing, and all the other formalities of good letter writing. A field trip to the post office would be a natural extension of this lesson.

This pen pal exercise goes on for two or three rounds before the enthusiasm wanes. It's great fun to watch the childrens' faces when they find a new letter in their cubby. Other characters that would be fun to hear from would be Goldilocks, Cinderella, Beauty, the Beast, Hansel or Gretel, or the Witch.

Other Topics for Spring Activities

1. Enjoy any seed planting activities. Now is a good time for the shoe garden activity on page 72.

2. Make butterflies. Have children work in pairs. One child lays his or her hands on a large piece of construction paper, wrists touching, while the partner draws the outline of the hands to suggest a large butterfly. Decorate.

3. Create ladybugs and other creepers. Paint halves of walnut shells with red paint. When dry, add seven black spots, using cotton-tip swabs for brushes. Create spiders from single egg-carton cups, using pipe cleaners for legs.

4. Study frogs and other amphibians.

5. Investigate turtles and other reptiles.

6. Learn about baby chicks and other members of the bird family.

7. Do an expanded unit on the oddities of Mother Nature, such as tornadoes, earthquakes, tsunamis and tidal waves, hurricanes, volcanos, blizzards, and droughts. Let the children work in teams to create a bulletin board titled "The Worst Day Ever."

8. Roll out clay into slabs a half inch thick. Trace and cut around each child's hand. Roll clay fingers up slightly into a cupped position. Fire in a kiln and present to mothers as soap or jewelry holders.

9. Do an expanded unit on conservation and ecology.

10. Have a tea party. Invite parents and the principal. Let some or all of the children tell about a particular unit of study. Celebrate spring!

11. Do an expanded unit on eggs.

12. Make pussy willow pictures by drawing a bare branch on a sheet of paper. Then get out a stamp pad and make buds by stamping ink on the branches with fingertips. Use red ink to make a few ladybugs and bees flying around, too. Fingerprint art is lots of fun.

13. Do a unit on rainbows.

14. Have each student practice addressing skills by writing his or her summer address on a postcard. Let them decorate the front of the cards. Surprise them this summer by dropping them a line on their very own postcards.

15. Buy some luscious strawberries as soon as they are in season and do a version of the popcorn game on page 72.

16. Have a pet show (only one dog at a time, please).

17. Have a "sleepover." Reserve the gymnasium for a Friday evening and invite parents and other family members to bring their sleeping bags and a good book. Everyone wears pajamas—even you—and lounges around reading to each other from 7:00 to 8:30. Then serve "breakfast" of juice and pastry and send everyone home. I sometimes use this opportunity to have my students put on a short talent show as well. This is one of our favorite springtime activities when the daylight evenings begin to get longer.

18. Cook and drain thin spaghettini noodles, spray muffin tins with oil, and create bird's nests in the cups. Dry for a week, remove, and create a papier-mâché bird from torn newspaper and wallpaper paste to sit on the nest.

19. Have children paint a spring landscape using only shades of green. They can use crayons, markers, colored pencils, watercolors, torn tissue paper, or tempera, but only in shades of green. The results will not disappoint them.

A School Year of Special Occasions

September

National Cat Health Month (make a cat book in the magazine center)

National Clock Month (create a clock and watch collection for a display)

National Sight-Saving Month (have fun reading an eye chart, look through a magnifying glass and a microscope)

National Popcorn Poppin' Month (see game on page 72)

First week—Emergency Care Week (learn how to clean and bandage cuts and scrapes)

Second Sunday—National Grandparents Day (make a card or painting)

Third Tuesday—International Day of Peace (absolutely no arguments this day)

Fourth Friday—Native American Day (learn an Indian child's game)

Fourth Saturday—Kids Day (report on Monday what you did Saturday)

September 13—Milton Hershey's birthday (1847) (pass out some chocolate Kisses)

September 16—The Mayflower left from Plymouth, England (read the story)

September 21—The first day of autumn (make a fall tree with torn paper)

September 22—Native American Day (learn about Sacagawea)

September 26—Johnny Appleseed's birthday (make applesauce)

September 27—Ancestor Appreciation Day (bring photographs of grandparents for a class bulletin board)

October

National Apple Month (do an expanded apple unit)

National Popcorn Month (do an expanded corn unit)

National Roller Skating Month (bring your skates to school for recess)

National Pasta and Pizza Month (make homemade noodles and sauce for a pasta party or evening parent involvement activity)

First week—International Children's Week (study children of another culture)

Second week—National Newspaper Week (do the kid's pages of your paper or create a class newspaper)

Fourth week—National Magic Week (teach everyone a few tricks)

October 8—Columbus Day (study ships of long ago)

October 10—Giuseppi Verdi's birthday (listen to *Rigoletto* or *Aïda* during the day)

October 13—White House completed in 1792 (draw the White House)

October 31—Halloween

November

International Creative Child Month (go for it! have a class art show)

First week—American Music Week (listen to a different country performer each day)

Third week—National Children's Book Week (draw a scene from your favorite book or make a diorama in a shoebox)

Fourth week—National Family Week (draw a family portrait; bring a parent to school)

November 4—King Tut's Tomb discovered (1922) (read Aliki, *Mummies Made in Egypt*)

November 6—John Philip Sousa's birthday (march around the room to "The Stars and Stripes Forever")

November 11—Veterans Day (what is a veteran?)

November 14—Claude Monet's birthday (look at some prints; paint one of your own in Monet's style)

November 17—Homemade Bread Day (bake some rolls in a toaster oven)

November 18—Mickey Mouse's birthday (make a pair of paper ears or study mice)

November 30—Mark Twain's birthday (read one of his great stories)

December

December 5—Walt Disney's birthday (rent a Disney classic video for the afternoon)

December 12—Poinsettia Day (make crêpe-paper poinsettias to wear)

December 16—Beethoven's birthday (listen to a great symphony)

December 17—Wilbur and Orville Wright flew their first airplane (do a little research on old airplanes or make a paper one to fly in the classroom)

December 21—First day of winter (create snowmen, see activity on page 123)

January

National Soup Month (everyone bring a vegetable and make stone soup)

National Hobby Month (bring a hobby to share)

January 1—New Year's Day

January 4—Louis Braille's birthday (1809) (explore some Braille materials with fingers)

January 5—George Washington Carver Day (do a mini-unit on his life)

January 16—National Nothing Day (make up a reason to celebrate)

January 27—Mozart's birthday (listen to another great piece of music)

February

National Cherry Month (make cherry tarts in a toaster oven)

American Heart Month (get a beef heart and dissect it—yes, really!; get a stethoscope and listen to each other's hearts)

Black History Month (study famous black Americans)

International Friendship Month (find a pen pal in another class)

National Children's Dental Health Month (bring in a dentist for a tooth-brushing lesson—ask your school nurse for help)

Second week—Crime Prevention Week (fingerprint your whole class on index cards)

February 2—Groundhog Day (how did this get started anyway?)

February 12—Abraham Lincoln's birthday (make a stovepipe hat and a fake beard; take a class picture of everyone in facial fur)

February 14—Valentine's Day

February 20—President's Day (put up pictures of all the presidents—ask the media technician for help)

February 22—George Washington's birthday (how many years ago was this? admire his picture on a dollar bill or a quarter)

March

Music in our Schools Month (ask your music teacher to help children make homemade instruments; play along to some pop music)

Red Cross Month (read the story of Clara Barton)

Youth Art Month (go for it! frame the great ones—frame them all)

National Women's History Month (study several ladies of renown)

National Nutrition Month

Good Health Month (list all the elements of good health)

First week—Save Your Vision Week (read about Helen Keller)

Third week—National Poison Prevention Week (study good versus bad drugs)

Third week—National Wildlife Week (go for a walk to find wild animals, especially little tiny ones under piles of dead leaves)

March 1—National Pig Day (cook some bacon; make BLTs; discuss where pork chops come from)

March 2—Dr. Seuss's birthday (create a Seuss-like character of your own and name it)

March 10—Harriet Tubman Day (read a story about her)

March 14—Albert Einstein's birthday (how many things could this man do? use an encyclopedia to find out)

March 21—Fragrance Day (have a blindfolded "Smells in a Jar" contest)

March 30—Happy Doctor's Day (call a pediatrician and sing "Happy Doctor's Day to You" from the kids at your school—he or she will love it!)

April

National Humor Month (everyone learn a good joke to tell to the class)

Keep America Beautiful Month (plant flower seeds in a foam cup)

Third week—Reading Is Fun Week (everyone read a short book to class or act out your favorite story)

Fourth week—National Library Week (learn to use the card catalog or create a cover for your favorite book)

Fourth week—National Week of the Ocean (make an ocean collage)

First Saturday—World Health Day (do the dirty potato experiment on page 101)

Fourth Monday—Earth Day (clean up your playground; clean out your desk)

April 1—April Fool's Day (watch out!)

April 2—Hans Christian Andersen's birthday (read a good fairy tale)

April 9—First elephant brought to the United States by P.T. Barnum (draw a circus scene)

April 22—Arbor Day (plant a tree, or at least draw one)

May

National Fitness and Sports Month (draw you doing your favorite sport)

American Bike Month (have a bicycle safety day with a police officer)

Better Sleep Month (tell about your best dream or your worst)

Older Americans Month (visit a retirement home and sing a few songs)

First week—National Photo Week (let the kids take pictures of each other making their silliest faces)

Second week—Teacher Appreciation Week (hope for a few nice notes)

Second week—Clean Air Week (study sources of pollution near your school)

Second week—Be Kind to Animals Week (visit a pet shop or Humane Society)

Third week—International Pickle Week (sample all the different kinds—yum!)

Second Sunday—Mother's Day (make a pop-up card)

Last Monday—Memorial Day (who will your family remember?)

May 1—May Day (make a May Basket for the principal)

May 3—International Tuba Day (bring in a high school tuba player)

May 4—National Kid's Workout Day (do some aerobics at recess today)

May 5—Cinco de Mayo (learn a Mexican dance or song)

May 5—Japanese Children's Day (make a paper kite to fly at recess)

May 18—International Museum Day (visit a local museum)

May 21—Peace Day (write a letter to the president or governor)

June

American Rivers Month (find the rivers in your state on a map; mark them with a highlighter)

Adopt-A-Cat Month (don't!) (learn cat expressions, like "You're the cat's pajamas," or "While the cat's away, the mice will play," or "Don't be catty!")

Second week—National Little League Baseball Week (have a ball game or a pitching contest today)

Third Sunday—Father's Day (write what's important about fathers or create a colorful paper tie for Dad to wear)

June 9—Donald Duck's birthday (walk around all day like a duck)

June 14—Flag Day (create a class flag)

June 21—First day of summer (ahhh! we made it!)

Conclusion

Cross-curricular units using a central theme are the stuff on which creativity thrives. I hope you will try a few of these suggested activities this year and let your imagination and those of your students soar. Refer to the outline when you feel stymied and the ideas will flow again. When former students come to visit me, I ask them what they remember most and invariably they mention activities that revolved around some central theme.

Resources

(Note: The asterisk [*] denotes titles I believe are most helpful to first year teachers.)

*Beckman, Carol, Roberta Simmons, and Nancy Thomas. *Channels to Children: Early Childhood Activity Guide for Holidays and Seasons.* Colorado Springs, Colo.: Channels to Children, 1982.

Butzow, Carol M., and John W. Butzow. *Science Through Children's Literature: An Integrated Approach.* Englewood, Colo.: Teacher Ideas Press, 1989.

Chapin, Laurie, and Ellen Flegenheimer. *Leaping into Literature.* Carthage, Ill.: Good Apple, 1990.

Collins, Cathy. *126 Strategies to Build Language Arts Abilities—A Month by Month Resource.* Needham Heights, Mass.: Allyn & Bacon, 1992.

Cornell, Joseph Bharat. *Sharing Nature with Children.* Nevada City, Calif.: Ananda Publications, 1979.

*Foster, Doris Van Liew. *A Pocketful of Seasons.* New York: Lothrop, Lee & Shepard, 1961.

*Haglund, Elaine J., and Marcia L. Harris. *On This Day: A Collection of Everyday Learning Events and Activities for the Media Center, Library, and Classroom.* Littleton, Colo.: Libraries Unlimited, 1983.

Harelson, Randy. *The Kids Diary of 365 Amazing Days.* New York: Workman, 1979.

Hofer, Kathy. *Year-Round Teacher Tips.* Huntington Beach, Calif.: Teacher Created Materials, 1991.

McElmeel, Sharron L. *My Bag of Book Tricks.* Englewood, Colo.: Libraries Unlimited, 1989.

Podendorf, Illa. *The True Book of Seasons.* Chicago, Ill.: Childrens Press, 1960.

Polette, Nancy. *The Research Almanac.* O'Fallon, Mo.: Nancy Polette, 1985.

Radlauer, Ruth Shaw. *About Four Seasons & Five Senses.* Chicago: Melmon, 1960.

Romberg, Jenean. *Let's Discover Tissue.* West Nyack, N.Y.: Center for Applied Research in Education, 1973.

Sandburg, Carl. *Chicago Poems.* New York: Henry Holt, 1916.

Schwartz, Linda. *Think on Your Feet.* Santa Barbara, Calif.: Learning Works, 1989.

*Sevaly, Karen. *Monthly Idea Book.* Riverside, Calif.: Teacher's Friend Publications, 1987.

*Vermeer, Jackie, and Miriam Laviuiere. *The Little Kid's Four Seasons Craft Book.* New York: Taplinger, 1974.

8
A Look Back and a Look Forward

In this last chapter I simply encourage you to take good care of yourself, celebrate your successes, get through this first year of assessment, holler for help when you need it, and enjoy every day that you spend with children. There is no best way to do anything, especially teach, and I urge you to find your most comfortable style and develop it throughout your career. Share your great ideas with others and learn from them, too. Take a class now and then just for yourself and not because you need it for recertification. Take a rest and recuperation day just for you when you need it. Get out of town or go on a shopping spree, spend the day with an old friend or a new one, or just stay in bed all day and don't answer the phone. Bring your renewed self back to your students and plunge in once again.

By all means, remember that you are only human—and only *one* human at that. You cannot change the lives of all of your students, but you can be the teacher they will remember fondly for the rest of their lives. You may never know the influence you have had on a child, or you may get a big surprise one day down the road when you see one of your children in the news doing something wonderful. Then you will know that it has all been worthwhile.

In a year or so, make a few phone calls to former students just to see how they are doing and to let them know that you still care about them. A good teacher's influence shouldn't end when June rolls around. The real rewards sometimes come years later when you least expect them. These casual phone and letter visits with children from the past are what keep adding fuel to my fire.

Your First Assessment

Your successes and weaknesses will be noted during this first year by your supervisors and principal through a formalized assessment program of one kind or another. You will be informed of these procedures before or soon after your first few days of school. Your first evaluation system may resemble this:

1. Orientation and training session at which you learn the responsibilities and the timelines for both you and the evaluator during the assessment process.

2. Definition of specific goals and objectives.

3. Scheduling of observation times and pre- and post-observation conferences.

4. Compilation of a remediation plan, if necessary.

5. Additional observations and review of remediation plan.

6. Final assessment review.

7. Building of a professional growth plan.

8. Approval for continuing employment in current or new position.

There are many variations on this procedure, but most districts have a similar plan for evaluating new teachers. You may have only your principal performing your evaluation, or you may have a team with as many as three other district educators involved. Keep in mind that you, and all teachers, are under scrutiny at all times by parents, students, peers, and the public in general. (My first teaching contract required that I never be seen smoking or imbibing in public places. It also stipulated that, should I become pregnant, I would submit my resignation at the end of my first trimester. Yes, baby, we *have* come a long way.)

Joining Professional Organizations

Most school districts have a local teachers' organization or union. You will soon be approached to join, and that decision is a highly personal one. These organizations are instrumental in negotiating a mutual master agreement with the local school board to improve teaching conditions, create equal employment opportunities, set calendars, settle disputes and grievances, and set salary standards. The union's strength depends on the number of employees it represents. It is financed by the dues paid, usually on a monthly basis, by its members. Typically, the local union also belongs to a state and a national organization. Ask fellow teachers any questions you have about your local organization—its longevity, services, past performance, benefits, and drawbacks—before making a decision about joining.

If you have a particular interest in specific content areas, consider joining organizations such as:

• International Reading Association, 800 Barksdale Road, P.O. Box 8139, Newark, DE 19714

• Association for Childhood Education International, 11501 Georgia Avenue, Wheaton, MD 20902

• National Science Teachers Association, 1742 Connecticut Avenue NW, Washington, DC 20009

Continuing Education

Just when you think you are finished taking classes and being a student yourself, you find out that you will have to undertake more studies to keep your teaching certificate current. Ask your principal what is required in your state and district to renew your certificate. Don't wait until six months before your expiration date to begin taking courses. Your teacher's lounge will be knee-deep in brochures on classes being offered by your district and local colleges and universities. Check the bulletin boards for upcoming classes and ask if you don't find such announcements.

There are now several colleges that bring instructors to a town or city for weekend classes. These are called *outreach programs*, and I have found them to be a refreshing change of pace from the usual night or summer classes. If you don't get yourself in a time crunch by putting off course work until the last minute, you can pick and choose classes that truly interest you.

Not all of your credits must come from a university, so you can take a few classes just for your own enrichment. Two of the best and most useful treats I have given myself in the past few years were a calligraphy class and a cartooning class. Not only did I thoroughly enjoy them, but the skills I learned have been more helpful to my daily teaching chores than some of my advanced classes in theory.

Know the requirements and plan long-range goals for your own particular tastes and needs. If you are floundering with math, by all means take another math methods class. Every instructor has gems you can use in the classroom. When you feel you know yourself and your goals more fully, look at options for obtaining a master's degree in a field of high interest for you and your future career. Take a class now and then from your local Parks and Recreation Department. You will meet new people in other fields of endeavor and keep your perspective on the world outside of school. Have a good talk with yourself once in a while to see where you've been, where you are, and where you're going. Then you can decide what classes will benefit you most.

Goals for Outstanding Teachers

In the following reproducible pages, you will find lots of food for thought as you go from day to day through this first year in the classroom. The teachers who really stand out in their fields are the ones who not only have a thorough understanding of the subject matter they present each day, but also demonstrate a deep understanding of the thinking and learning processes of their students. Every day will be a learning experience for you as you gain new insights into your own psyche and those of the children in your charge. Seek out other teachers you admire and learn their secrets for success. Ask a million questions and acknowledge your insecurities. Most veteran teachers will be happy to give gentle advice and reassure you by sharing their "first-year" stories. One day you will be the one helping a new teacher. You have unique and creative ideas of your own and now you finally have a chance to try them out. Read these lofty goals often and before long they will become second nature to you.

Goals for Outstanding Teachers

Class Climate

◆ I have created a friendly, pleasant environment in which my students appear to be relaxed and comfortable. I ask for their input and suggestions to make our classroom more inviting. My students feel free to bring things from home to promote ownership of their school space.

◆ I am supportive and accepting of individual differences. I provide ample time for my students to discuss individual problems. I am always asking and looking for new ways to help my special students.

◆ My interaction with students is positive, encouraging, and uncritical. I am careful not to let sarcasm creep into my dealings with children. My students feel safe and accepted in our class.

◆ I give the children many opportunities to contribute to the physical climate of our classroom by helping to design bulletin boards, class decorations, and displays.

◆ All children have ample opportunities to have input into decision making regarding classroom rules and curriculum choices.

Productive Use of Time

◆ Minimal time is spent on such noninstructional tasks as attendance, paperwork, bathroom breaks, transition time to new subjects, and so on.

◆ My classroom space is well organized. I look over my classroom each afternoon to see if changes are needed. I rearrange seating assignments frequently to allow for variety in social and learning interaction and to avoid boredom.

◆ My students function independently to get the materials they need. I periodically review the procedures I expect them to follow.

◆ My materials are prepared in advance. My daily lessons are clearly defined in my mind. I give myself a few minutes each afternoon to see that the next day's materials are ready and available. I arrive early enough each morning to make last-minute preparations.

◆ I give concise directions for each new activity. I check verbally and visually every few minutes to see that everyone is still focused on their assignments.

◆ I spend a minimum of time in transition from one activity to another. I assist children who have difficulties with transitions, knowing that this is a confusing process for some.

◆ My students understand our daily routine. I make changes in our schedule as needed and review often to provide maximum feelings of security.

Classroom Management

◆ I stated my expectations the first day and carried through consistently. I have written my expectations in my plans for my substitutes so that there is always continuity in my classroom when I have to be away.

◆ I keep rules to a minimum. I always say what I mean and mean what I say.

◆ My students clearly understand expected behaviors. They can count on me to be fair and consistent with everyone in our class. I don't play favorites.

◆ I watch for the necessity to restate and reteach. When more than three children need help with their independent work, I know I have not been clear with my directions.

◆ Parents are aware of my behavior management policies. I have sent them written statements of my behavior management techniques and have been prompt to call for conferences when needed, before problems escalate.

Instructional Presentation

◆ I review and check for prior knowledge before each lesson or activity. I ask what children already know about each new topic to eliminate redundant information and get a feel for their interests.

◆ I give an overview of each lesson and why it is relevant. I try to provide a hands-on experience for each lesson that cements knowledge and gives meaning for use in everyday life.

◆ I monitor to see that all students are attending. I use body language and nonverbal communication to recapture lost attention. I am aware of childrens' signals indicating that it is time for a break or a subject change.

◆ I frequently model the expected outcome of a lesson. I try never to forget to think like a child and take the time needed to amplify each experience. I mentally break down each lesson to visualize each component clearly before presentation.

◆ I use concrete examples when appropriate. Whenever possible, I encourage children to role play and reteach for me.

◆ I present my lessons in an organized, step-by-step manner, checking frequently for comprehension of each new concept with appropriate questions.

◆ I use a variety of teaching modes for each new concept. Do some of my students learn best by hearing, seeing, feeling? I ask myself, "How can I teach this lesson in another mode?"

◆ I ask for frequent feedback from the students. I often ask children to repeat what I have just taught in their own words, or I ask them to reteach the lesson to the class.

◆ I give my students guided practice opportunities. I allow the children to use the overhead projector or chalkboards to show what they have learned or would like to share with their classmates.

◆ I check my pacing frequently to see that everyone understands. My lesson plans are in pencil and show flexibility by occasional erasures and additions.

◆ I use student errors as an opportunity to reteach, but never single out or identify any child's work so as to cause embarrassment.

◆ I present new lessons with obvious enthusiasm. I approach each topic as though it is all new and exciting to me. My body language and voice attest to my joy in new discoveries.

◆ My lessons are varied and of high interest. They often reflect suggestions from my students and those students are invited to share in the teaching or reviewing.

◆ My lessons encourage critical thinking, problem solving, decision making, and independent learning.

Progress Evaluation

◆ I move about the classroom continually, checking individual progress. I reteach whenever necessary.

◆ I regularly confer with children. My students know when they can speak privately with me.

◆ I keep good records of each child's progress in all areas and share this information in a timely manner with each child.

◆ I observe students' on-task time continuously and give verbal feedback.

◆ I consult with each student about goals and progress. We make decisions about pieces to be placed in the student's portfolio.

◆ I give students opportunities to have input into grading criteria. I use an informal report card created jointly by the students and me.

◆ I give children the responsibility and opportunities to self-evaluate and improve performance by conferencing, making and reviewing portfolios, and co-planning curriculum choices.

◆ I keep parents informed of positive, as well as negative, performance. I make it a point to phone or write to parents about good things that are happening with their children.

Personal Relationships

◆ I communicate with students, staff, parents, and community in a professional and productive manner.

◆ I cooperate with staff members in planning and executing shared responsibilities.

◆ I promote student development and express respect for myself and others.

◆ I treat all students with respect and dignity.

◆ I keep parents and staff informed of class activities and involve them when appropriate.

Professional Growth

◆ I take classes as needed to increase my expertise in appropriate curriculum areas.

◆ I join committees within my building and district to further my understanding of educational goals for students.

◆ I read professional journals and magazines to stay current on methods and issues.

◆ I maintain records and lesson plans to document my preparation and results.

Personal Objectives

◆ I maintain professional ethics and confidentiality. I discuss personal information with appropriate staff members only.

◆ I am open to learning from others and accept constructive criticism graciously.

◆ I freely offer new ideas and methods to peers.

◆ I strive to be a role model for students, parents, and peers.

◆ I allow myself the freedom to take time whenever needed to maintain my mental and physical well-being.

Conclusion

Most of your children will be open to all of your new ideas and very resilient to your mistakes. You *will* make a lasting impression on them, for better or for worse. That is the choice you must make each morning when you enter your classroom. Most primary students will see you as a saintly being and it is your task now to become worthy of their adoration and respect. I am a little envious of, and at the same time sympathetically concerned for, the journey you are about to begin. Teaching in the twenty-first century will be a challenge that I cannot even begin to imagine. I am grateful that I was a product of the "Happy Days" era and entered this profession when teachers were still put on pedestals by students, their parents, and the community. I hope you will find a way to help reinstate our profession in its rightful place of high regard. I am feeling the winds of change in education and I know that the task before you is much more difficult than any I have experienced, so I offer my best wishes to you for the strength and dedication you will need in the times ahead. I hope I was able to calm some of your fears and inspire you just a little. Enjoy each moment with your children and every day of your wonderful career, because your life will never be same again.

Resources

Curwin, Richard L., and Barbara Schneider Fuhrmann. *Discovering Your Teaching Self.* Englewood Cliffs, N.J.: Prentice-Hall, 1975.

Krajewski, Robert J., and R. Baird Shuman. *The Beginning Teacher: A Practical Guide to Problem Solving.* Washington, D.C.: National Education Association, 1979.

Appendix
Food for Thought:
Helping Your Child at Home

The *Food for Thought* pamphlet on the following pages is designed for you, the teacher, to photocopy and hand out to your students, their parents, or your peers (other teachers), for in-service programs and other educational programs in a single school. There is nothing that would please me more than for this pamphlet to exhibit the wear and tear of repeated use.

You will discover many simple, easy-to-make projects in this pamphlet that will help children with reading, math, spelling, and thinking. By trying just one idea per week, you will be helping them to become more successful students. It will make a difference!

You may make as many photocopies as you please (on any color of paper!), but the pamphlet must be photocopied in its entirety (to conform to the guidelines of its copyright).

Have fun!

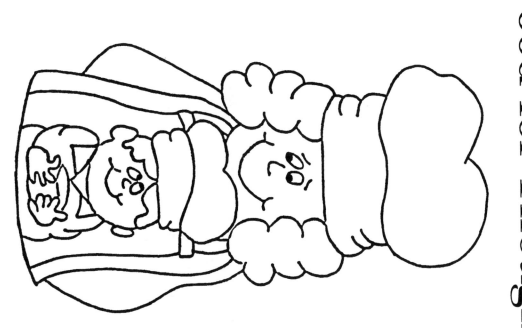

Food for Thought

Helping Your Child at Home

by Memory Schorr

MRS. SCHORR'S
BEST EVER FUN-DOH

1 cup of water
½ cup of salt
1 cup of flour
1 tablespoon oil*
2 teaspoons of cream of tartar

Mix together all ingredients in a sauce pan. Cook about 2 minutes until thick. Cool 10 minutes and play. Wrap tightly and store in the refrigerator. It will last for months.

*add food coloring

Dear Parents and Teachers:

In this "cookbook" you will find many simple, easy-to-make projects that will help children with reading, math, spelling, and thinking.

By trying just one idea per week, you will be helping them to become more successful students. Encourage the children to engage in more imaginative play, outdoor activities, interaction with other children, and less television viewing.

Ten to fifteen minutes per day spent with a child reading or playing one of these games will make a difference in each child's learning rate. I think you will enjoy putting these projects together with your children, using materials found in your home or at school. I welcome your feedback. Have fun!

Memory Schorr

From *A Handbook for First Year Teachers: Ready! Set! Go!* by Memory Schorr.
© 1995. Teacher Ideas Press. Englewood, Colo. (800) 237-6124

From *A Handbook for First Year Teachers: Ready! Set! Go!* by Memory Schorr.
© 1995. Teacher Ideas Press. Englewood, Colo. (800) 237-6124

MEAT TRAY WORD FIND

Use a marker or crayon to divide a meat tray into sections. Write one letter in each space. Be sure to include a few vowels (a-e-i-o-u). Have children look for as many words as possible by moving a finger from space to space. Letters that form words must be touching left to right, right to left, up and down, or diagonally.

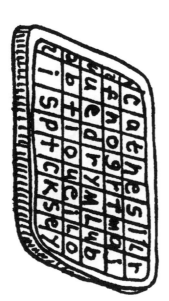

FOODS IN A "FLASH"

1. Clip food pictures from advertisements in newspapers or magazines.

2. Glue the advertisements to cardboard to make flashcards.

3. Have children categorize

   a. by fruits, vegetables, meats, dairy, breads, junkfoods, and so on

   b. by colors

   c. by sweet—unsweet

   d. by cooked—uncooked

   e. by eaten hot—eaten cold

   f. by nutritious—not nutritious

   g. by animal—vegetable

   h. by likes—dislikes

   i. by expensive—inexpensive

4. Have children find the names of the foods in print and then match them to the pictures.

WORD BANK

Make a "word bank" for the sight words or spelling words children learn at school. Paste the words to cardboard and cut into coin shapes. Write a value on the back of each word. Place them in a discarded milk jug like the one here. Empty the words one-by-one from the "jughead." As each child says a word, he or she also adds up the values. Children are practicing their reading and math skills, and you are recycling a milk container!

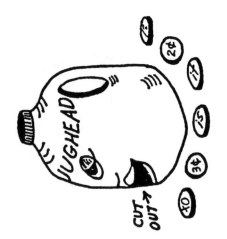

From *A Handbook for First Year Teachers: Ready! Set! Go!* by Memory Schorr.
© 1995. Teacher Ideas Press. Englewood, Colo. (800) 237-6124

TABLE-TOP-TAPPING

Tap out rhythms with a kitchen utensil on a table or a pan. Have your child or student copy your patterns. For instance:

_____ (pause) _____ _____ (pause)

_____ (pause) _____ (pause)

(pause) _____ _____ (pause)

Vary the sounds and patterns by using drinking glasses filled with different levels of water—or several pots and pans. These activities help children to improve their auditory memory.

From *A Handbook for First Year Teachers: Ready! Set! Go!* by Memory Schorr.
© 1995. Teacher Ideas Press. Englewood, Colo. (800) 237-6124

KITCHEN TOOL MATCH-UP

Trace the outline of several kitchen utensils on paper or cardboard. Have children match the utensils to the outlines.

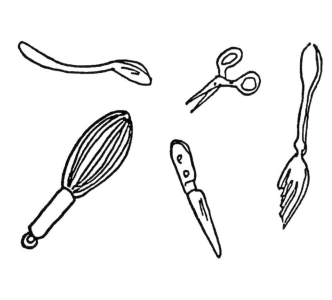

LETTER FIND

Put a few canned goods or food packages on a table for children to study. Have them do an alphabet count of the letters on each label. Some packages that might be used are Campbell's soup or Rice-a-Roni boxes. Your letter count might look like this:

A-15	D-0	G-?	J-?	M-?
B-0	E-16	H-?	K-?	N-?
C-0	F-3	I-?	L-?	

Do the entire alphabet, then ask questions like: Which letter was used most? Least? Not at all? Only once? Twice? Three times? Which letters were largest? Smallest? What colors were used? And so on.

TIME TO RHYME

Play rhyming games with your child or student based upon objects found around the house or class-room.

POT-(HOT)   BOOK-(HOOK)

SPOON-(MOON)   PEN-(HEN)

DISH-(WISH)   BELL-(WELL)

CHALK-(TALK)   PLATE-(DATE)

Children might even like to start a scrapbook of rhyming words. Find pictures in old magazines.

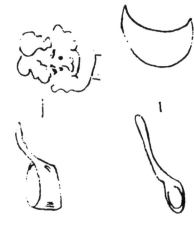

From A *Handbook for First Year Teachers: Ready! Set! Go!* by Memory Schorr. © 1995. Teacher Ideas Press. Englewood, Colo. (800) 237-6124

MAGIC SLATE

Put about a half cup of hair gel or cheap hand lotion in a plastic, self-sealing kitchen storage bag. Add a few drops of food coloring, seal tightly, mix thoroughly, and smooth out. Instant magic slate!

Write on it with a fingertip or pencil eraser. Kids can practice handwriting, spelling words, or math facts in a fun way.

From A *Handbook for First Year Teachers: Ready! Set! Go!* by Memory Schorr. © 1995. Teacher Ideas Press. Englewood, Colo. (800) 237-6124

PAPER PLATE SPINNERS

Divide a large piece of round paper, or a plastic plate, and a small plate into sections with a marker or crayon. Fasten through the center with a brad. Write action words (verbs) in the small plate sections and word endings in the outer parts of the larger plate.

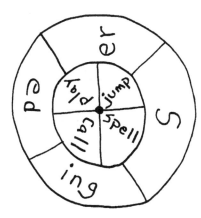

Have children spin the small plate. Read the words and use the words in sentences. They could also act out the words, or spell them with beans or alphabet noodles.

TOOTHPICK CONSTRUCTIONS

This activity is fun for the whole family or class. Use toothpicks and raisins, miniature marshmallows, soaked garbanzo beans, or soft candies to create constructions of all kinds. A plastic foam meat or bakery tray makes a good base to build on. Also, have your child or student construct letters or numbers in the same way.

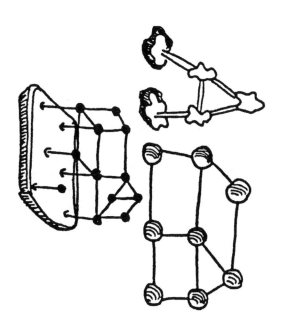

KITCHEN GARDENERS

Try growing grass or sprouting seeds in some of these ways: Put a little dirt or a piece of discarded sink sponge in half an eggshell. Draw a face on the side of the shell. In a few days you will have an "egghead!" Or, cut a potato in half, scoop out a little and plant with seeds. Cut an old sponge into an interesting shape, moisten, and sprinkle with seeds.

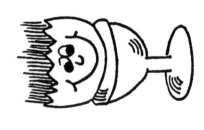

Try growing avocado seeds, onion, a carrot top, a potato with "eyes," a pineapple top, or a sweet potato. Plastic foam egg cartons filled with a little soil make handy kitchen gardens, too.

From *A Handbook for First Year Teachers: Ready! Set! Go!* by Memory Schorr. © 1995. Teacher Ideas Press. Englewood, Colo. (800) 237-6124

PAPER ROLL
BOWLING MATH

Save toilet paper rolls for a few weeks and you will soon have enough to make a fun math game for children to play. Write a number on the side of each roll. Set the rolls on end like bowling pins and have each child roll a ball at them. Ask them to add up the numbers on the ones they knock down each time.

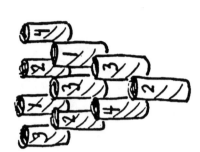

From *A Handbook for First Year Teachers: Ready! Set! Go!* by Memory Schorr. © 1995. Teacher Ideas Press. Englewood, Colo. (800) 237-6124

ALPHABET NOODLES

Alphabet noodles, sold in the pasta section of the grocery store, make a great teaching tool for a variety of reading, spelling, or math activities. Use cooked or uncooked. Practice for spelling tests. Learn new or difficult words. Practice alphabetical order.

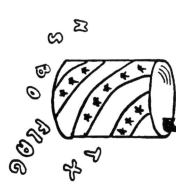

Leftover noodles can be stored in empty salt containers that children have decorated.

PHONICS BINGO

Use a plastic foam meat tray and a marker to make a listening bingo game. Mark the letters of your bingo game on the tray.

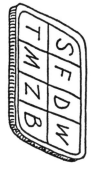

S	F	D	W
T	M	Z	B

Give children some beans, pennies, raisins, or markers of some kind. Enunciate the beginning sounds of words so that each child can hear and tell you the letter he or she hears first. Like this:

s-s-salt   f-f-first   d-d-doll
m-m-me   t-t-tall   w-w-work

With the beans, pennies, or raisins, each child covers the letter-sound he or she correctly identifies. Reverse roles. Your child or student sounds out words and you cover the letters. This game will quickly improve reading and spelling.

LIMA BEAN SPELLING

Use a marker to write the alphabet on large beans. Store them in a jar or plastic container marked "SPILL THE BEANS." These beans can be used for a variety of activities:

1. Practice spelling words
2. Make up a crossword
3. Put in alphabetical order
4. Spell out family names
5. Give children all the letters in the spelling word, but scramble them and have the children figure out the word by unscrambling.

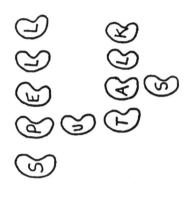

From *A Handbook for First Year Teachers: Ready! Set! Go!* by Memory Schorr.
© 1995. Teacher Ideas Press. Englewood, Colo. (800) 237-6124

CATEGORIES

There are many activities children can do centered around categories.

1. Give children a few old magazines. Have them cut out pictures that belong to certain categories (e.g., people, animals, fruit, or clothing).

2. Give children several sheets of paper titled bathroom, bedroom, kitchen, living room, garage, and backyard. Have them cut out pictures and paste them on the appropriate page.

3. Cut out pictures that start or end with the same sound (e.g., baby, banana, bike; or, bed, bread, sled, salad).

4. Have children make a scrapbook of a variety of categories. Here are just a few. Things that are:

tiny	hot	round	red
huge	cold	square	green
drinks	toys	tools	animals

5. Start a game of Categories at the dinner table or in the classroom. Have each person take turns adding new items to a specific category. Naming the states is a good one.

From *A Handbook for First Year Teachers: Ready! Set! Go!* by Memory Schorr.
© 1995. Teacher Ideas Press. Englewood, Colo. (800) 237-6124

GRAPH GAMES

These are fun for the entire family or class. You can give points for each square filled. Each person has a graph with his or her name in the grid across the top. Fill the side grid with categories.

I am...	M	A	R	K
I like to play with	marbles	art stuff	roller skates	kites
I like to eat	marsh-mallows	apples	rice	kiwi
Favorite Animal	monkey	ants	rabbit	kanga-roo
Favorite Color	mid-night blue	?	red	?

I am...	L	O	R	I
Food	lobster	Oreos	ribs	ice cream
flower	lily	?	rose	iris
Jobs	land-lord	office worker	race car driver	jet pilot
states	Loui-siana	Ohio	Rhode Island	Indi-ana

MY OWN DESK

A large cardboard box from the grocery store is free and can easily be made into a sturdy study and play desk for a child at home. A smaller box can be made into a little seat for the new desk. Everyone needs a place for his or her own stuff!

SYMMETRY

1. Cut a large magazine picture in half.
2. Paste on paper.
3. Ask children to complete the missing half of the picture with crayons or markers.
4. Alternate using the left and right halves of pictures.

From *A Handbook for First Year Teachers: Ready! Set! Go!* by Memory Schorr. © 1995. Teacher Ideas Press. Englewood, Colo. (800) 237-6124

CUBBYHOLES

Old oatmeal and salt cannisters and plastic containers of all kinds make great storage cubbyholes for school supplies, papers, or art supplies. They can be easily painted or covered with wallpaper scraps, sticky paper, Sunday's comics, and magazine pictures. Glue or tape them together to make a pyramid.

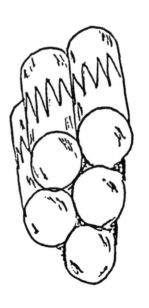

From *A Handbook for First Year Teachers: Ready! Set! Go!* by Memory Schorr. © 1995. Teacher Ideas Press. Englewood, Colo. (800) 237-6124

COMIC STRIP CUT-UPS

Comic strips can help children become familiar with a series of events and sequencing. Sunday comics are best because they are larger and more colorful. Cut them apart, have children arrange them in order, and then help them read.

JIGSAW PUZZLES

1. Paste a large magazine picture to some cardboard.
2. Write something about the picture at the bottom.
3. Cut up the picture jigsaw style.
4. Have children reassemble the picture and read it to you.

NAME EVERYTHING!

On a piece of paper, write down the names of objects in your child's room or in the classroom. Cut out the names and pin or tape them to the objects. For instance: window, curtain, ceiling, floor, door, dresser, bed, closet, shelf, toy box, and so on.

This is a wonderful way to show young children the meaning of the written language at an early age. Older children will enjoy doing this activity by themselves. Spelling will improve with this one!!!!

SURPRISE MESSAGES

Write notes to children that are easy to read and put them in unexpected places for them to find. Some places might be:

lunchbox
backpack
under a pillow
jacket pocket
cookie jar
refrigerator
in a favorite toy
under a dinner plate
in a pajama pocket
in the mailbox

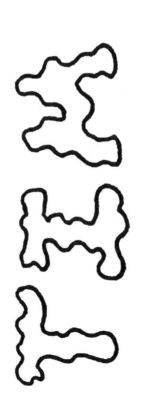

See you at 5:00!

I miss you!

See you after school!

sweet dreams

We are so proud of YOU!

I need a hug!

I.O.U. XXX

Have a nice lunch!

Have a GREAT day at school!!

I love you

From *A Handbook for First Year Teachers: Ready! Set! Go!* by Memory Schorr. © 1995. Teacher Ideas Press. Englewood, Colo. (800) 237-6124

LATHER WRITING

Use bargain shaving cream foam to practice reading, writing, spelling, and math on a table or counter (or even in the bathtub!). Write children's names with the foam and have them spread it out into a smooth layer. Then have them practice any subject by writing in the foam with a fingertip or pencil eraser. (Bonus: You get a clean table and hands!)

From *A Handbook for First Year Teachers: Ready! Set! Go!* by Memory Schorr. © 1995. Teacher Ideas Press. Englewood, Colo. (800) 237-6124

MEMORY GAME

Place a variety of small objects in the egg spaces, one per space. Have children study the objects for a minute and then close the egg carton. Ask them to name all of the objects in the carton. Even harder, where were they? Can you do it?

TRAVELING EGG CARTON

This activity is played while riding in a car. Glue slips of paper with letters on them into the bottom of the egg spaces. As you are traveling along the road, look for objects that begin with sounds in your egg carton. When one is spotted, for example, a gas station, give your child a cereal piece to put in the G letter space. When an entire row is filled, they can eat all the cereal and begin again.

COLOR OR SHAPE MATCH

Cut out colored eggs or circles, squares, and triangles (2 of each) and play a similar matching game in the egg carton.

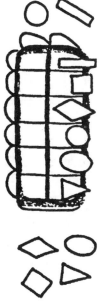

NUMBERS

Practice counting by writing numbers on egg shapes. Put "number" eggs in the top row of the egg carton and have children put a corresponding number of raisins or cereal pieces in the matching space. You could also play this game with buttons, pennies, etc.

EGG CARTON GAMES

Cut egg shapes from colored paper or cardboard (52 pieces). Write all of the capital letters and small letters on the egg shapes. Have children choose 6 capital letters and place them in the top row of the egg carton. Then have them find the matching small letters.

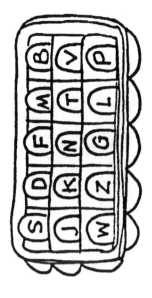

To keep track of how many correct answers they give, reward each child with a raisin, peanut, or a piece of cereal for each correct match.

From *A Handbook for First Year Teachers: Ready! Set! Go!* by Memory Schorr. © 1995. Teacher Ideas Press. Englewood, Colo. (800) 237-6124

EGG CARTON GRAPHING

Help children think of interesting Yes or No questions to ask family members or classmates. For instance: Do you like spinach? Can you stand on one leg for a minute? Have you ever seen a skunk? Write the question on a piece of paper and place it in the lid of the egg carton. Write Yes and No on slips of paper and attach to the sides of the carton. Have children place some raisins or cereal bits in the correct row of the egg carton as they question family members or classmates. Afterward, they can announce the results of the survey by looking for the row with the most filled sections.

EGG CARTON COMPUTERS

Glue egg cartons together to make a typewriter or computer keyboard for children to play with or to practice spelling words on. Kids really do love these! Cut out circles of cardboard for the letters and glue them to each end of the egg compartments. An empty paper towel roll glued to the top makes a great pretend paper holder.

From *A Handbook for First Year Teachers: Ready! Set! Go!* by Memory Schorr. © 1995. Teacher Ideas Press. Englewood, Colo. (800) 237-6124

Index

About the Author

Memory Long Schorr has been a classroom teacher for the past 34 years (18 years with physically handicapped students, 8 years teaching second grade, and the past 8 years as a Chapter I Communication Arts teacher). She currently teaches at Washington Elementary School in Colorado Springs, Colorado.

Memory received her Bachelor of Science in Elementary and Special Education from Illinois State University, and Master of Arts in Education from Lesley College. She is a past board member of United Cerebral Palsy, and has designed and conducted numerous college classes and in-services for new and veteran teachers in Colorado and Illinois.

In 1987, Memory was the recipient of the Colorado Distinguished Teacher Award. More recently she received the 1994 Governor's Award for Excellence in Education from Governor Roy Romer of Colorado and the Colorado Endowment for the Humanities, and was named 1994 Reading Teacher of the Year by Soroptimist International of Colorado Springs.

Memory has four children and four grandchildren, and lives in Manitou Springs, Colorado, with her husband, Larry.